1,000
FACTS
YOU JUST WON'T
BELIEVE

First published by Parragon in 2013

Parragon
Chartist House
15–17 Trim Street
Bath BA1 1HA, UK
www.parragon.com

ISBN 978-1-4723-1152-8

Printed in China

1,000 FACTS YOU JUST WON'T BELIEVE

PaRragon

Bath • New York • Singapore • Hong Kong • Cologne • Delhi
Melbourne • Amsterdam • Johannesburg • Shenzhen

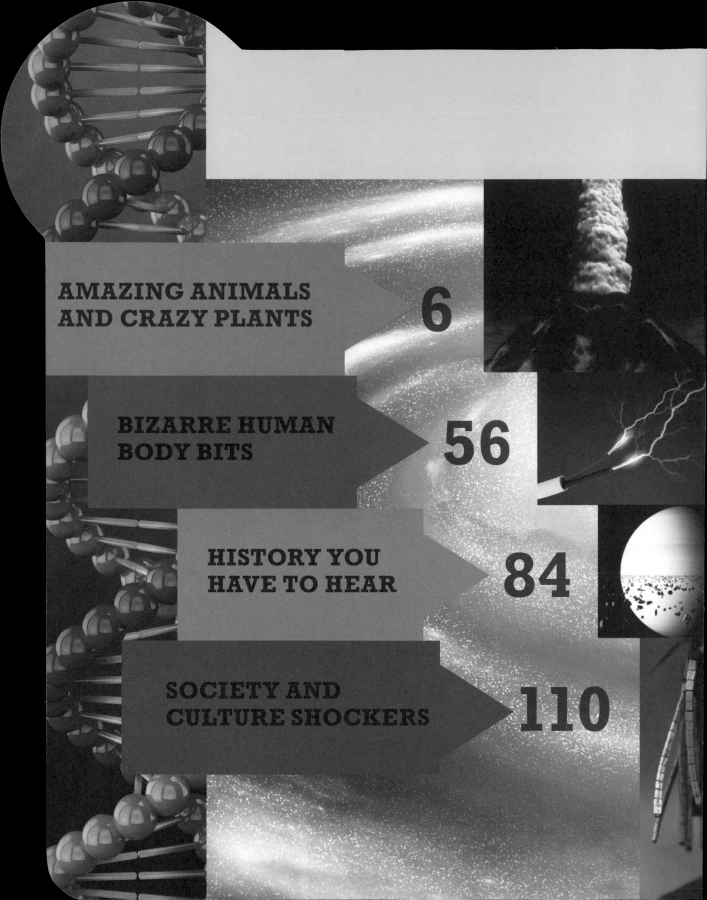

WHAT'S INSIDE?

AMAZING ANIMALS

ANIMALS AND

CRAZY PLANTS

A **SIX-YEAR-OLD** could stand inside a **HIPPO'S MOUTH** when it's wide open. #0001

The star-nosed mole has **22** tiny "fingers" on its snout, for **touching** and feeling its way around. #0002

Ostriches' **eyes** are bigger than their **brains.** #0003

Do you **JUMP** when you get a **FRIGHT?** An **ARMADILLO** does—straight up in the air, more than 3 feet high. #0004

5 DEADLY ANIMALS

HIPPOS kill more people every year than sharks, bears, lions, or leopards. #0005

A **GOLDEN POISON DART FROG** is so poisonous that you could die from just touching it. #0006

You can tell when a **BLUE-RINGED OCTOPUS** is about to deliver a **DEADLY BITE**—bright blue rings suddenly appear all over its body. #0007

The **BOX JELLYFISH**, the most venomous creature on Earth, is almost invisible in water. #0008

NEEDLEFISH sometimes leap out of the water and accidentally stab fishermen with their **SHARP SNOUTS.** #0009

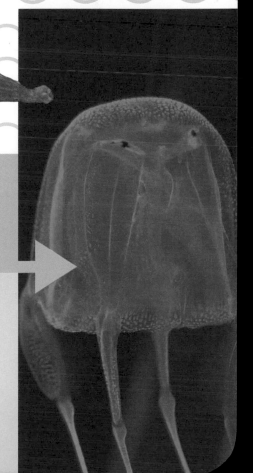

A **BOOTLACE WORM** found on a Scottish beach measured

164ft.

That's as long as

30

people lying end-to-end. #0010

10 BONKERS BIRD FACTS

A **swift** can stay in the air for **over 3 years** without landing on the ground! #0011

A **bee hummingbird** weighs less than a **cent.** #0012

The **male satin bowerbird** decorates his nest with any **blue** objects he finds. #0013

The **hooded pitohui bird** has **deadly poison** in its skin and feathers. #0014

An **owl** can't move its eyes, but it can **rotate its head** to face backward. #0015

A **bald eagle's nest** can be as big as a **garage!** #0016

Fieldfares scare off enemies by **dive-bombing** them with their **poop!** #0017

If you scare a **fulmar chick,** it can squirt fishy, oily **vomit** into your face from **10 feet away.** #0018

A **wood pigeon's** feathers weigh more than its bones. #0019

The **emperor penguin** can dive **1,640 feet.** That's more than the height of most skyscrapers. #0020

3 FACTS ABOUT SOMETHING FISHY...

Blobfish, which are jellylike deep-sea fish, sit on their **eggs** until they hatch, just like chickens. #0021

FLASHLIGHT FISH have two glowing **LAMPS** on their heads. They can use them to attract food and "talk" to each other over long distances. #0022

The **whale shark** is the **biggest** fish. It's gentle and friendly to humans! #0023

4 SAFARI SNIPPETS

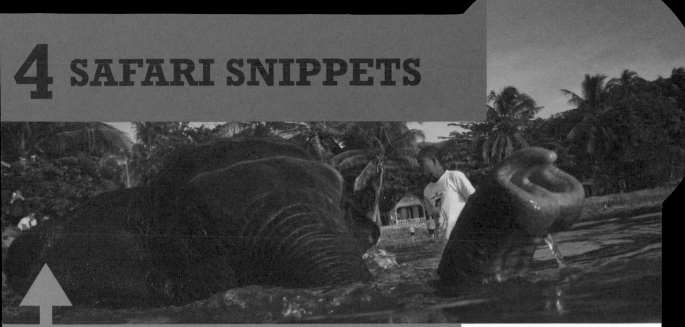

Elephants use their trunks as **snorkels** when they walk or swim under water. #0024

BLACK RHINOS have such bad **EYESIGHT,** they sometimes charge at trees and termite mounds by mistake. #0025

Hippos whirl their tails around to spray their **poop** over a wide area and mark their territory. #0026

A **GIRAFFE'S** kick is so powerful that it can **KILL A LION.** #0027

10 CREEPY FACTS ABOUT SEA CRITTERS

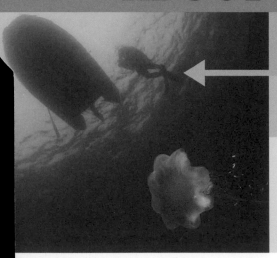

The **lion's mane jellyfish** can have tentacles **100 feet** long. #0028

A **sea cucumber** can excrete its internal organs to reduce in size! #0029

When a **pistol shrimp** snaps its claw, it makes a noise as loud as a jet engine, and heats the water nearby to **7,200°F.** #0030

One single **hagfish** can turn a whole bucket of water into **slime** in minutes by releasing horrible mucus from its body. #0031

The **dresser crab** wears **camouflage.** It covers itself with bits of seaweed, sponges, and other sea creatures. #0032

All **clownfish** are born **male,** but some later change into **females.** #0033

The **barreleye fish** has a see-through head, with its eyeballs buried deep inside it. It looks through its own head to see! #0034

To eat, **starfish** turn their **stomach inside out** and wrap it around their food. #0035

Handfish walk on the seabed with fins that **work like legs.** #0036

The **deep-sea giant isopod** looks like a **woodlouse,** but is much bigger! #0037

3 SLITHERING SNAKE FACTS

A **spitting cobra** can shoot venom straight into your eyes from **6.5 feet** away. #0038

Rattlesnakes gain an extra ring for their **rattles** every time they shed their skin. #0039

A **reticulated python** is big enough to swallow a **human** whole! #0040

If a predator grabs a **GECKO'S** tail, the tail falls off and **WRIGGLES AND SQUEAKS.** This confuses the predator so the gecko can escape! #0041

5 AWESOME OCTOPUS FACTS

The **MIMIC OCTOPUS** can imitate the shape of a flatfish, a jellyfish, a stingray, a seahorse, or a deadly sea snake. #0042

An octopus has **THREE HEARTS** and **NINE BRAINS**—one main brain and a smaller one for each of its tentacles. #0043

Octopuses can change **SHAPE, COLOR, AND TEXTURE,** so they can pretend to be a speckled rock, bumpy coral, or frilly seaweed. #0044

The deep-sea **DUMBO OCTOPUS** is like the cartoon elephant because it has massive flappy "ears" (which are actually fins). #0045

An octopus can distract predators by squirting an **INK CLOUD** that creates an octopuslike shape. #0046

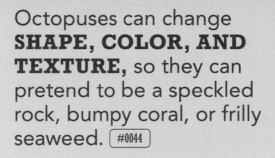

4 EVEN MORE BONKERS BIRD FACTS

A **woodpecker** can peck **20 times** in just one second. #0047

Cassowaries can kick so hard with their claws, they can slice through a car door. #0048

Tiny birds called **swiftlets** make nests out of spit. People sometimes collect the nests and use them to make **soup!** #0049

FLAMINGOS eat with their heads **UPSIDE-DOWN.** #0050

A **blue whale** is bigger than **any dinosaur** ever discovered! #0051

A blue whale can hear another blue whale singing from **over 900 miles** away. #0052

Whales can't breathe through their **mouths,** only through their **blowholes.** #0053

Bottlenose dolphins can wrap **sea sponges** around their noses to protect them from sharp rocks. #0054

A **humpback whale** can have so many barnacles living on it that they alone weigh as much as six men. #0055

Sperm whales stun their prey by blasting it with an incredibly loud **cracking sound.** #0056

Some Amazon River dolphins are **bright pink!** #0057

Baby whales have hands before they're born. The fingers fuse together to create their fins. #0058

Whales' closest living relatives are **hippos.** #0059

A **Pacific white-sided dolphin** can leap out of the water up to **30 feet** high! #0060

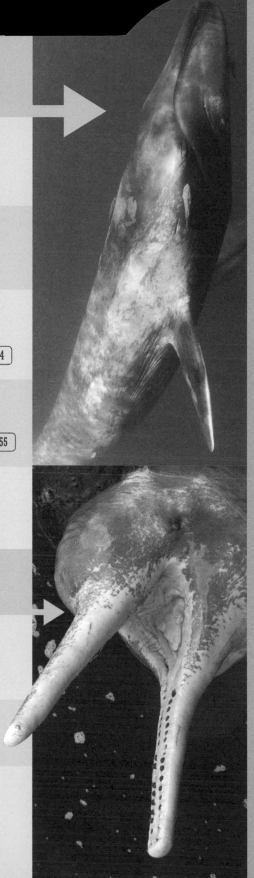

5 ASTONISHING ANT FACTS

An **ANT** can carry an object that's **20 TIMES** its own weight. That's like you carrying a car! #0061

In Africa, colonies of over **20 MILLION SAFARI ANTS** march together in a huge procession. They are so powerful that even elephants get out of their way! #0062

Some ants capture ants from other nests to use as their **SLAVES.** #0063

HONEYPOT ANTS spend their lives hanging on the ceiling of a tunnel inside their nests, using their globe-shaped bodies to hold food for other ants in the colony. #0064

The **bullet ant** has the most painful sting of any insect—it feels like **being shot** and the pain can last for 24 hours! #0065

3 SHOCKING RAT FACTS

Rodents' **teeth** never stop **growing**—they have to gnaw constantly to grind them down. #0066

Rats dribble a trail of **pee** everywhere they go. #0067

The giant **BOSAVI WOOLLY RAT,** discovered in 2009, is as big as a cat. #0068

10 JAWDROPPING SHARK FACTS

Tiger sharks eat **almost anything.** Some things found inside their stomachs include:

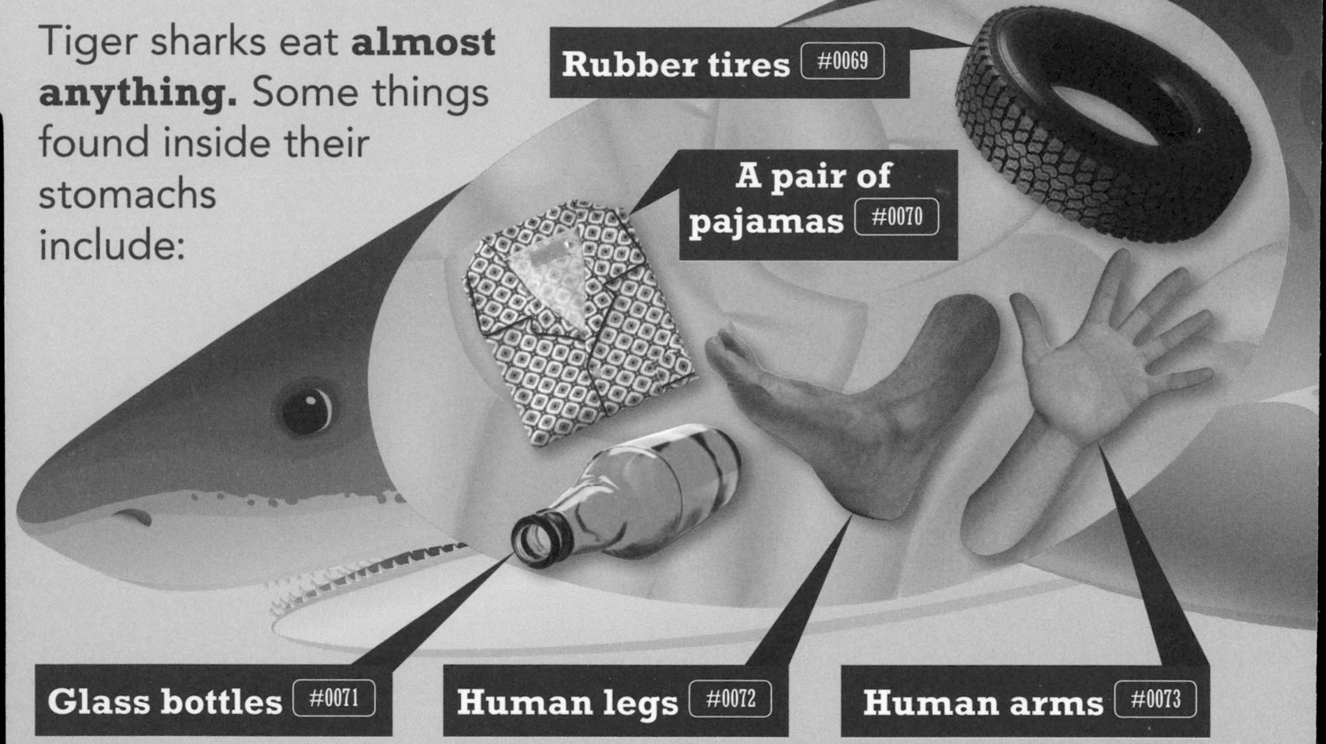

Rubber tires #0069

A pair of pajamas #0070

Glass bottles #0071

Human legs #0072

Human arms #0073

Sharks' **skin** isn't scaly, or smooth either—it's covered in **tiny tooth-shaped spikes.** #0074

Sharks have no bones—their skeletons are made of **rubbery cartilage.** #0075

Sharks do **spiral-shaped poops.** #0076

A shark wouldn't really enjoy eating you. They usually **only attack humans by mistake**. #0077

Sharks kill around **20 humans** a year, but humans kill **100 million sharks.** #0078

The **CHICKEN** is the most common bird in the world. There are about **SEVEN** chickens for every human on the planet. #0079

10 SUPER-POWERED ANIMAL SENSES

Sharks can sense the **electrical signals** animals' bodies give off when they move. [#0080]

A male emperor moth can smell a female from **6 miles away.** [#0081]

A **pit viper snake** has heat-sensing "pits" on its face that allow it to detect its prey's body heat. [#0082]

A **rat's whiskers** are so sensitive, they can pick up sound vibrations in the air. [#0083]

Giant pouched rats can be trained to **sniff out** land mines and certain diseases. [#0084]

When **flies** land on food, they have a quick taste—using the tastebuds on their feet! [#0085]

Camels can close their **ears and noses** to protect themselves in a sandstorm. [#0086]

Some **butterflies** have **ears on their wings,** to listen for bats that want to eat them. [#0087]

Octopuses can taste and smell with their **suckers.** [#0088]

A **chameleon** can point its eyes in **two different directions** at the same time. [#0089]

Goats and sheep have **rectangular pupils** to help them see sideways. #0090

The **shy-eye shark** covers its eyes with its fins when it sees a bright light. #0091

All **domestic dogs,** however different they are in size, belong to the **same animal species.** #0092

The **DEADLIEST** creature on Earth is the **MOSQUITO.**

It spreads deadly diseases such as malaria, which kills **HUNDREDS OF THOUSANDS** of people every year. #0093

10 BABY ANIMAL BRAINTEASERS

An **ostrich egg** is so **strong** that you could stand on it without breaking it. #0094

Mice breed so fast that in one year, two mice can multiply to become over **4,000 mice.** #0095

A newborn baby **kangaroo** is smaller than your **thumb.** #0096

The greatest number of **yolks** ever found in one chicken **egg** is nine. #0097

Giraffes give birth standing up, so their babies fall **6.5 feet** onto the ground. Ouch! #0098

A **Surinam toad's** babies hatch out from under the skin on her back. #0099

Sand tiger sharks often start to **eat each other** inside their mom's body before being born. #0100

Baby **tortoise beetles** put predators off by covering themselves in their own poop. #0101

Baby **periodical cicadas** can live for **17 years** underground, yet once they become adults, they live only a **few weeks.** #0102

Baby **elephants** greet each other by **intertwining trunks** and like to play chasing games! #0103

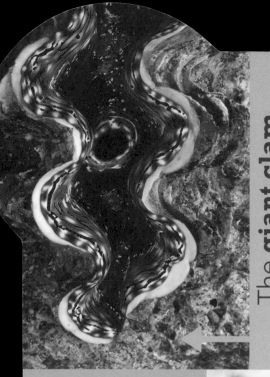

The **giant clam** can grow as **big as a couch.** #0104

The **colossal squid** has the **biggest eyes** of any animal. Its eyeballs are the size of basketballs! #0105

ROBBER CRABS can **CLIMB TREES** and crack open coconuts for a snack. #0106

MANTA RAYS can jump up to **10 FEET** out of the sea and flap their fins like wings as they "fly." #0107

5 FUNGI FACTS

The super-deadly **DEATH CAP TOADSTOOL** looks very like the tasty, **EDIBLE STRAW MUSHROOM.** #0108

Just one mushroom can release **BILLIONS OF SPORES** (tiny fungus seeds). #0109

Fungi can grow in soil, on old wood, around bathtubs—or **ON YOUR FEET AND TOENAILS!** #0110

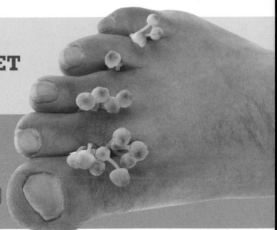

Some mushrooms, such as **STINKHORNS,** smell of **ROTTING MEAT,** or even **POOP.** The smell attracts flies, which then spread their spores. #0111

A fungus known as **"WINTER WORM, SUMMER GRASS"** invades a caterpillar's body in winter (so it looks like a worm), then grows out of its brain in summer (so it looks like grass). #0112

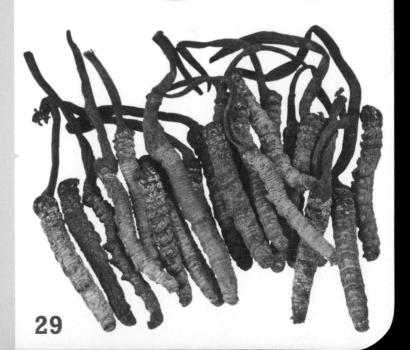

3 PECULIAR PREHISTORIC FACTS

In prehistoric times, there were **giant dragonflies** the same size as some modern eagles. #0113

The **closest living relatives** of the dinosaurs are, in fact, **BIRDS!** #0114

Until a living **coelacanth fish** was caught in 1938, scientists thought they had been **extinct** for 65 million years. #0115

10 INCREDIBLE INSECT FACTS

A **quarter** of all animal species are **beetles.** #0116

Antarctic springtail bugs can **reduce their temperature** for the winter. #0117

Bees are found on every continent except Antarctica. #0118

Some **flies** have their eyes located on eyestalks that are longer than their bodies. #0119

Glasswing butterflies have **see-through wings** that look like glass. #0120

"Millipede" means "1,000 legs"—but the millipede with the most legs actually has only **750.** #0121

A large **praying mantis** can catch, kill, and eat a **mouse.** #0122

Fireflies can **flash** their glowing tails on and off to send each other **messages.** #0123

In her whole lifetime, a **worker honeybee** makes less than one tenth of a teaspoon of honey. #0124

A **dragonfly** can zoom along at almost **40 miles per hour**—faster than a **tiger** can run! #0125

Plant **roots** are so tough that they can break through **concrete.** #0126

Giant **AMAZON WATER LILY PADS** are strong enough for a **CHILD** to stand on. #0127

A **bristlecone pine tree** in California is thought to be around **4,800 years** old—and it's still growing. #0128

The **BEE ORCHID FLOWER** looks just like a real **BEE.** #0129

5 BLOOD-SUCKING BAT FACTS

VAMPIRE BATS really do drink blood from people and animals.
#0130

The **BUMBLEBEE BAT,** the world's smallest bat, is actually smaller than some bees. #0132

Using **ECHOLOCATION** (bouncing sounds off objects and detecting the echoes), bats can locate an object as thin as a human hair. #0133

Bracken Cave in Texas has a colony of **20 MILLION BATS** living in it.
#0131

Bats' wings are made from skin stretched between their **FINGERS.**
#0134

10 SENSATIONAL SPIDER AND SCORPION FACTS

Scorpions **glow in the dark!** If you saw one in the light of the Moon, it would look neon blue. #0135

The **brown recluse spider's** venomous bite eats away at human flesh, leaving a hole that takes weeks to heal. #0136

Most spiders have **eight eyes,** but the **Kauai cave wolf spider** doesn't have **any.** #0137

Spider silk is so strong that a spider silk rope as **thick as a pencil** could stop a **jet aircraft.** #0138

Spiders often recycle their silk by **eating their old web** before spinning a new one. #0139

The **biggest spiderweb ever found** covered a line of trees 192 yards long in Texas. #0140

Baby spiders make parachutes, to float away from their nest, from threads of spider silk. #0141

Scorpions can't sting themselves—they are **immune** to their own **poison.** #0142

A thread of spider silk long enough to reach around the whole world would weigh **less than this book.** #0143

Spiders can spin webs while floating in space. #0144

The **LYREBIRD** can **IMITATE SOUNDS** it hears exactly—including at least **20** other birds' songs, frog calls, and even chainsaws, camera shutters, and car alarms. #0145

Horseshoe crabs have **bright blue blood!** #0146

CHEETAHS living in desert areas survive without drinking water by eating **MELONS.** #0147

DOGS began living and working with humans more than **30,000 YEARS AGO.** #0148

Wolves have webbed toes. #0149

The **flying fox** isn't a fox—it's a **giant bat,** with wings that can be almost **6.5 feet** across. #0150

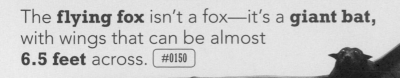

Bar-headed geese fly over the Himalayas at up to **26,250 feet**—almost as high as Mount Everest. #0151

Hummingbirds can beat their wings so fast that they appear **invisible.** #0152

The wandering albatross can have a **11.5-foot wingspan,** so each wing is as long as an adult human. #0153

Flying fish use their fins as wings to glide distances of **590 feet** through the air. #0154

To **fly like a bird,** we would need wings as big as dinner tables! #0155

One type of tiny **midge** can beat its wings more than **1,000 times every second.** #0156

The **longest recorded flight** of a **chicken** is **13 seconds.** It flew just over 110 yards. #0157

A **swarm of flying locusts** can contain **10 billion** insects, and be so thick it blocks out the sunlight. #0158

In 1973, a **Ruppell's vulture** flew into an aircraft at an altitude of **36,000 feet**—the highest bird flight ever recorded. #0159

5 LUDICROUS LIZARD FACTS

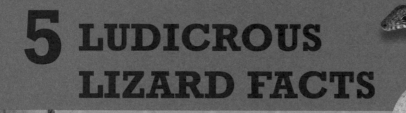

KOMODO DRAGONS sometimes dig up human graves looking for a snack. #0160

When threatened, **HORNED LIZARDS** squirt **BLOOD** from their **EYES** to confuse predators. #0161

Geckos can cling onto ceilings using thousands of tiny hairs on their **FEET**. #0162

A **CHAMELEON** can flick out its tongue to **6 INCHES** long in one thirtieth of a second. #0163

BASILISK LIZARDS can run on water. #0164

A fully grown tree produces **ENOUGH OXYGEN** in one year to keep a **FAMILY OF FOUR** breathing.

#0165

10 SUPER-SMART FACTS ABOUT ANIMALS

An **African gray parrot** named Alex learned to count, sort out **shapes,** and say 150 different words. #0166

Kanzi the **bonobo,** a type of chimpanzee, can understand around **3,000 English words.** #0167

A clever crow named Betty worked out how to make a **wire hook** to fish food out of a jar. #0168

Chimps poke sticks into termite nests, wait until termites crawl onto them, and then lick them clean. #0169

Some **Japanese macaques** wash potatoes in seawater to clean them and add salty seasoning. #0170

Ants can use their antennae to tell other ants how to **solve a maze.** #0171

Bonobos use plants and minerals as **medicines** to treat worms, diarrhea, and stomachache. #0172

Killer whales have been found to enjoy looking at **books!** #0173

An **octopus** can open a **screwtop jar** with its tentacles. #0174

An **elephant** can recognize itself in a **mirror.** #0175

Sociable **weaver birds** use grass to build huge nests with space for **200 or more birds.** #0176

How many times have you moved houses? **ORANGUTANS** build themselves a new **NEST** of leaves and branches **EVERY NIGHT!** #0177

When **BEAVERS** build a **DAM,** they can completely change the **DIRECTION OF A RIVER.** #0178

A **giant squid's esophagus** (the tube that food passes through to get to the stomach) runs right through its **brain.** #0179

Termite nests can tower up to **30 FEET TALL.**

That's about

eight times

the size of an average eight-year-old. #0180

10 FACTS ABOUT HUNGRY HUNTERS

Velvet worms shoot streams of **sticky glue** on their prey to trap them. #0181

The **tarantula hawk wasp** stings a tarantula to paralyze it, then lays its egg on it. When the wasp baby hatches, it eats the tarantula alive! #0182

The **death adder** wiggles the tip of its tail to look like a **tasty worm,** then when birds and lizards come to eat it, the adder eats them! #0183

Wild cats called **margays** can make a noise like a baby monkey. When the mother comes to look for her baby, the margay attacks! #0184

Killer whales sometimes **surf right out of the sea** and up onto the beach to grab their seal dinner! #0185

The **green heron** drops insects or bits of bread onto the water to lure **tasty fish** to the surface. #0186

Tigers in the Sundarbans area of India enjoy **snacking on humans!** They catch fishermen by sneaking up on them from behind. #0187

Net-casting spiders throw a special **net made of silk** over passing insects to trap them. #0188

The **stonefish** disguises itself as a stone, then grabs passing prey in its mouth in less than one tenth of a second. #0189

The **goliath tigerfish** of the Congo River is so fierce, it even attacks crocodiles! #0190

5 FACTS ABOUT INCREDIBLE JOURNEYS

ARCTIC TERNS migrate from the Arctic to the Antarctic and back every year, flying **44,000 MILES.** #0191

SALMON are born in streams, then swim all the way to the ocean. Before they die, they swim back to the **EXACT SAME STREAM** they came from to lay their eggs. #0192

MONARCH BUTTERFLIES can find their way to the very same spot where their great-great-grandparents hatched out. #0193

COCONUTS have been known to float **6,000 MILES** across an ocean before growing into a tree on another continent. #0194

Every spring, millions of **RED CRABS** on Christmas Island in the Indian Ocean migrate from forests to the **SEA** to breed. A few weeks later, their babies migrate back again! #0195

PLATYPUSES and **ECHIDNAS,** furry and spiny burrowing creatures found in Australia and New Guinea, are the only **MAMMALS** that lay **EGGS.** #0196

Three-toed sloths have moths living in their fur. #0197

Sea-slugs are **hermaphrodites**— they have both male and female reproductive organs. This increases their chances of finding a mate! #0198

Cow farts and burps produce around 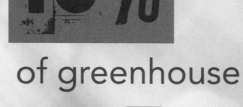 **10%** of greenhouse gases. #0199

Each animal has its own **collective noun**—a special name to describe a group of the same species:

A **MURDER** of crows #0200

A **LEAP** of leopards #0201

A **PRICKLE** of porcupines #0202

An **UGLY** of walruses #0203

A **MESS** of iguanas #0204

A **PARLIAMENT** of owls #0205

A **MURMURATION** of starlings #0206

A **KNOT** of toads #0207

A **CARAVAN** of camels #0208

A **KINDLE** of kittens #0209

4 BLINK-AND-YOU'LL-MISS-THEM CAMOUFLAGE FACTS

Leaf insects look like **LEAVES.** They have holes and brown patches to make their camouflage more realistic. #0210

The **OWL BUTTERFLY** has bright eye spots that make it look like an **OWL'S FACE.** #0211

The **swallowtail butterfly caterpillar** avoids being eaten by resembling a **bird dropping.** #0212

Stick insects trick predators because they look like **walking twigs,** and often their eggs look like seeds. #0213

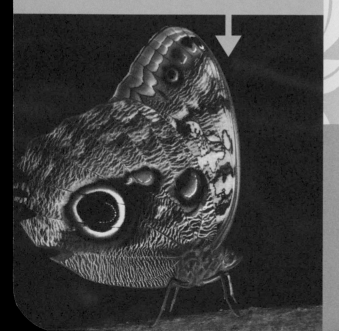

5 FACTS ABOUT MONKEYING AROUND

GORILLAS make burping and grumbling noises when they are **HAPPY.** #0214

Gorillas sometimes eat their own **POOP!** #0215

The **PROBOSCIS MONKEY** has a huge droopy nose, the biggest of any primate. #0216

Monkeys always peel **BANANAS** before they eat them—from the bottom end, not the stalk end. #0217

JAPANESE MACAQUES use natural hot springs to enjoy a **WARM BATH.** #0218

The heaviest insect, the **GIANT WETA,** weighs up to

3
ounces.

That's as much as a satsuma. #0219

10 PLANT-TASTIC FACTS

When **maple trees** are attacked by insects, they release chemicals into the air, to warn other trees. #0220

Pebble plants in the desert hide from hungry animals by looking exactly like stones. #0221

A **squirting cucumber** explodes to shoot seeds and slime up to **20 feet** through the air. #0222

The castor bean plant makes a **poison** so deadly, one teaspoon of it could kill **hundreds of people.** #0223

One **baobab tree** in South Africa has such a huge, thick trunk that a drinks bar has been built inside it. #0224

The **meat-eating giant pitcher plant** from the Philippines has traps so large it can swallow a **rat.** #0225

A single **banyan tree** can have **hundreds** of trunks. #0226

A **bamboo stalk** can grow more than **3 feet** in a single day. #0227

Giant redwoods are the world's tallest trees, reaching **375 feet** high, with trunks 16 feet across. #0228

The massive **titan arum flower** of Indonesia can reach **10 feet tall**—and smells like rotting meat! #0229

Tarantulas flick itchy hairs at their enemies. #0230

Scientists who study bugs (entomologists) have discovered **over 5,000 species of dragonflies.** #0232

An **electric eel** can give you a **shock** as bad as one from an **electricity socket at home.** #0231

4 CREEPY CRAWLY FACTS

Centipedes have a **poisonous bite** and a bite from the biggest ones can be dangerous to humans. #0233

A FLEA can jump more than 100 TIMES ITS OWN HEIGHT into the air. #0234

GIANT AFRICAN LAND SNAILS, which grow up to **10 INCHES LONG,** are a popular food in some countries. #0235

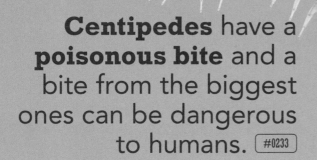

Earthworms are both male and female at the same time! #0236

A **fish tapeworm** can grow inside a human's intestines! #0237

The **cordyceps fungus** compels an ant to climb to the top of a grass stalk, before growing out of its head and releasing its spores. #0238

Boxer crabs carry around stinging **sea anemones** to sting their enemies! #0239

A **tongue-eating louse** eats a fish's **tongue,** then takes its place and lives within the fish's mouth! #0240

As a **tick** sucks blood from its host, it grows up to **10 times** its original body size. #0241

The biggest **bloodsucking leeches** are as long as your arm and as wide as a banana. #0242

Honey guide birds lead **honey badgers** to bees' nests. The badger breaks open the nest and the bird gets a share! #0243

The **cuckoo** lays its egg in another bird's nest, then that bird raises the cuckoo chick! #0244

A **leech** can suck up to **10 times** its weight in blood. #0245

Sharks let **pilot fish** swim inside their mouths to clean their teeth! #0246

54

TIGERS love **SWIMMING!**
However, they hate getting water in their eyes, so to keep their head dry they will often get in the water backward. #0247

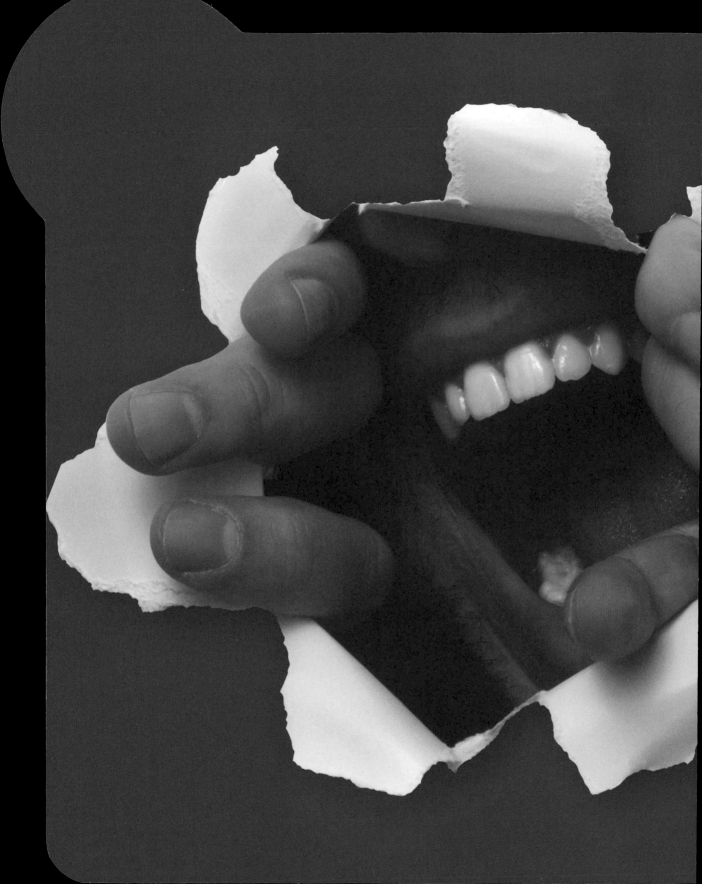

Chapter 2

BIZARRE
HUMAN
BODY
BITS

The loudest **SCREAM**
on record was

129 decibels.

That's as loud as a

Everyone has their own **smell** (except identical twins, who share a smell). #0249

Women **blink** twice as often as men. #0250

Humans are the only animals known to **cry** when they are sad. #0251

5 MAGNIFICENT MUSCLE FACTS

The muscle that exerts the most pressure for its size is the masseter or **JAW** muscle. #0252

You have to use about **300 MUSCLES** just to stand up without falling over. #0253

Astronauts' muscles get **WEAKER** the longer they spend in space. This is because their muscles don't have to work to resist gravity. #0254

The biggest muscle in the body is the **GLUTEUS MAXIMUS,** or **BUTTOCK.** #0255

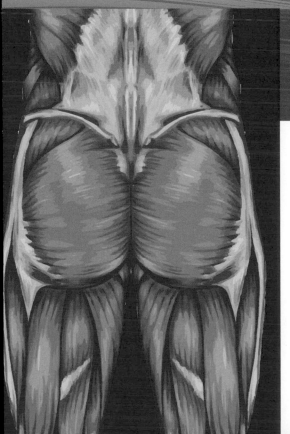

DIMPLES are caused by muscles pulling on the skin of your face. #0256

59

If all the blood vessels in your body were laid out in a line, they would reach **twice** around the world. #0257

10 TOUGH BONE FACTS

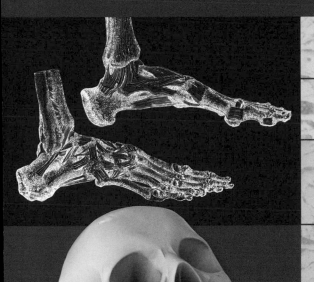

Human bone is stronger than **concrete** or **steel.** #0258

You have over **200 bones** in your body… #0259

… and **over half** of those are found in your **feet and hands.** #0260

People used to **drill holes in their skulls** to cure headaches. #0261

The ancient Aztecs used human thighbones to make **musical instruments.** #0262

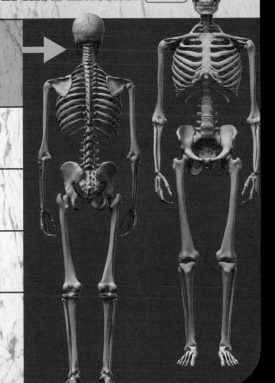

The rest of the body rots away after death, but bones can last for **thousands of years.** #0263

After the age of about 30, people's skeletons start to **shrink.** #0264

The **smallest bone** in your body is in your ears. It is less than **⅛ inch.** #0265

Your **bones** can repair themselves if they get broken, but your teeth can't. #0266

Your **funny bone** isn't actually a bone. It's a sensitive nerve running past your elbow joint. #0267

4 SNOOZY SLEEP FACTS

Some **SNORES** are as loud as a road drill. `#0268`

You spend around a **third** of your life fast **asleep.** `#0269`

When you **dream,** you don't invent people's faces —they are all people you've seen before! `#0270`

The record for a human lasting without sleep is **18 DAYS, 21 HOURS AND 40 MINUTES.** `#0271`

Today people can have artificial **LEGS, ARMS, FEET, NOSES, HEARTS, HIPS, TEETH, EARS,** and **HANDS.** #0272

10 THOUGHT-PROVOKING BRAIN FACTS

The human brain can do about **100 trillion** (100,000,000,000,000) calculations per second. #0273

If you spread the wrinkly covering of your brain out flat, it would be as **big as a newspaper.** #0274

If someone cut into your brain with a **knife,** you wouldn't feel any **pain.** #0275

There is evidence that a person can remain conscious for a few seconds after having their **head chopped off.** #0276

A normal human brain can store more information than a **room full of books.** #0277

If **half** of your brain was removed... you could live quite normally! #0278

A newborn baby already has all of its brain cells. #0280

The brain can shrink up to **15%** as it ages. #0279

U.S. scientist Chet Fleming has invented a device for keeping **a severed human head alive.** (It hasn't been built yet!) #0281

The brain works harder when you're **asleep** than when you're awake. #0282

Lee Redmond of Utah grew her **FINGERNAILS** to almost a

yard
LONG.

(Unfortunately they were then broken off in a car accident!) #0283

5 WEIRD THINGS THAT HAVE BEEN FOUND INSIDE PEOPLE'S STOMACHS:

COBBLESTONES #0284

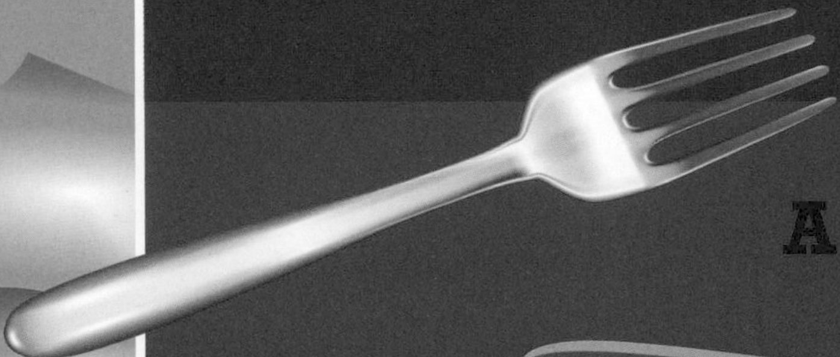

A FORK #0285

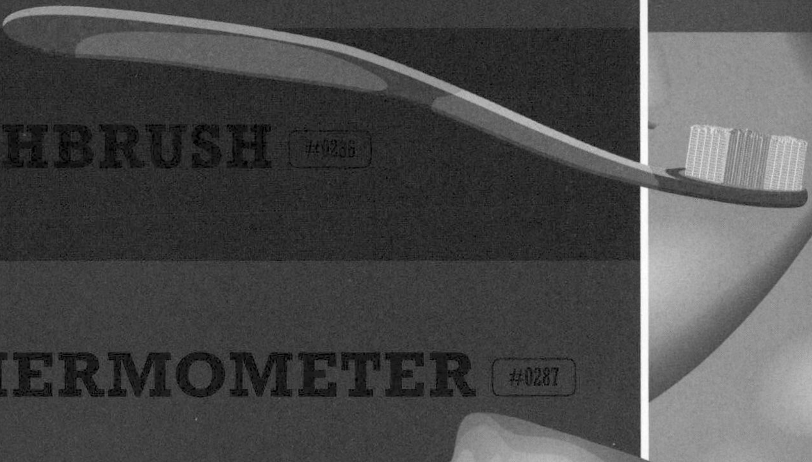

A TOOTHBRUSH #0286

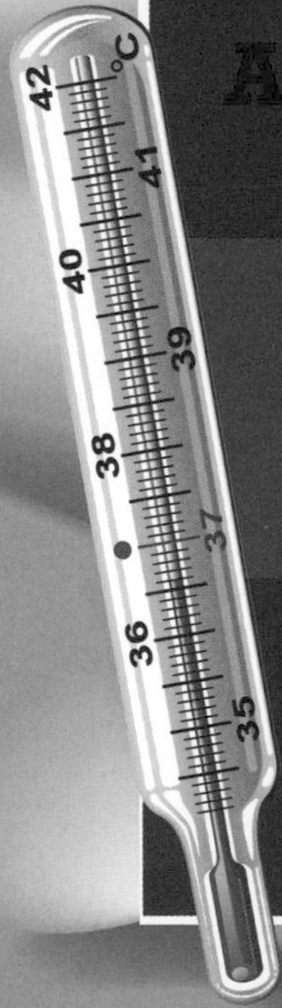

A THERMOMETER #0287

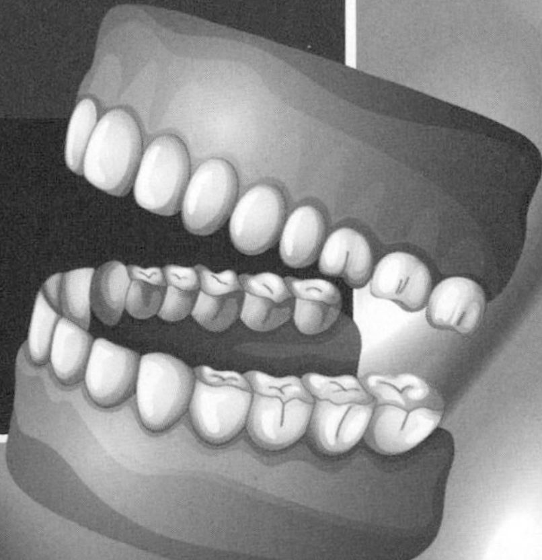

A SET OF FALSE TEETH #0288

3 FANTASTIC FINGER FACTS

If you **stretch your arms wide,** the distance between your fingertips is the same as your height. #0289

Your fingers have no muscles. (They are controlled by **muscles** in your arms.) #0290

Some people have **five fingers** and **one thumb** on each hand. #0291

In 1848, a railroad worker named Phineas Gage survived having an **iron bar blown though his brain** by an explosion. He lived until 1860. #0292

People with **synesthesia** get their senses mixed up—they may see sounds, feel colors, or taste musical notes. #0293

A man grows about **16.5 feet** of **beard** hair in a lifetime. #0294

10 HIGHLY SENSITIVE SENSES FACTS

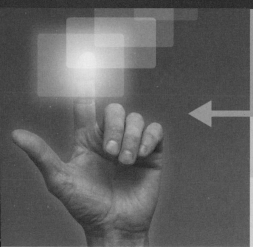

When you touch something, a message zooms from your fingers to your brain at **93 miles per hour**—as fast as a **speeding train.** [#0295]

Some people can **pop their eyeballs** right out of their head. [#0296]

You can't **taste** things if your tongue is **dry.** [#0297]

People who've lost an arm or a leg sometimes feel pain as if it's still there. It's called a **"phantom limb."** [#0298]

Children's **hearing** is better than adults'. [#0299]

Some blind people can sense where objects are by using **echolocation,** like bats do. [#0300]

Your nose can remember **50,000** different scents. [#0301]

Human eyes can detect over **a million** different **colors** and **shades.** [#0302]

All your life, your **nose** and **ears** very slowly keep getting **bigger...** [#0303]

... but your **eyeballs** stay almost the same size for your whole life. [#0304]

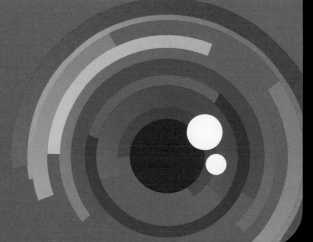

You are **TALLER** in the morning.

That's because **Gravity** squashes your body slightly during the day. #0305

5 THINGS DOCTORS HAVE MISTAKENLY LEFT INSIDE PEOPLE'S BODIES AFTER SURGERY:

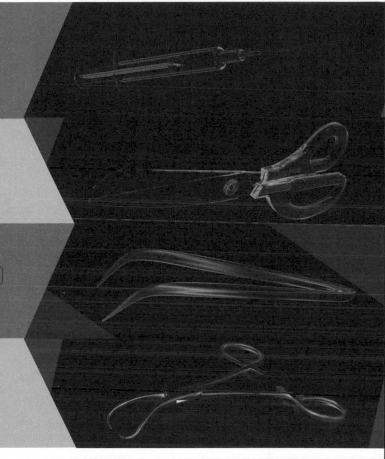

NEEDLE #0306

SCISSORS #0307

TWEEZERS #0308

PLIERS #0309

SPONGE
(This is the most common thing to be left behind, and can cause serious health problems.) #0310

10 BAFFLING BLOOD AND BREATHING FACTS

Your **heart** will beat between **2 and 3 billion** times over the course of a lifetime. #0311

If you spread all the breathing surfaces inside your lungs out flat, they would be the size of a **tennis court.** #0312

With every breath, you take in **air molecules** breathed out by **dinosaurs.** #0313

On deep dives without breathing equipment, a diver's lungs shrink to the size of **grapefruits.** #0314

Some people who've had **heart transplants** say they start liking the same food, hobbies, and colors as their heart donor. #0315

The **heart muscles** squeeze so hard they could squirt blood **30 feet** through the air. #0316

Blood is as salty as **seawater.** #0317

It takes about **45 seconds** for a blood cell to zoom around the body. #0318

Blood cells are made inside your **bones.** #0319

Octopuses have **blue blood** and insects have **yellow blood.** #0320

You make enough **SALIVA** each day to fill five teacups. #0321

Urine is germ-free and would be **safe to drink.** Not that you'd want to! #0322

If the **body's temperature** drops below **70° F,** it's usually fatal. #0323

4 LITTLE FACTS ABOUT LITTLE PEOPLE

More babies are born on a **TUESDAY** than on any other day. #0324

Babies start **dreaming** before birth. #0325

Babies are born with around **300 bones,** but by adulthood only 206 are left. #0326

Babies are born able to **swim** and to hold their breath underwater. #0327

5 BODY INGREDIENTS

An average human body contains enough:

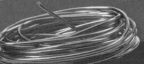

COPPER
to make
nearly half an inch
of thin copper
wire #0328

CARBON
to make
15,000 pencils #0330

ALUMINUM
to make
a piece of foil the size
of your palm #0331

IRON
to make
a large nail #0329

ARSENIC
to kill a rat #0332

Francesco Lentini

had

3

LEGS.

#0333

4 TINY CELL FACTS

The human body contains around **75 TRILLION** cells.

#0334

A typical human cell is **10 microns** across —about the size of a single speck of talcum powder.

#0335

The **longest cells** in the body are **nerve cells** reaching from the toes to the spine.

#0336

In the time it takes to read this sentence, **30 million** of your cells have died and been replaced.

#0337

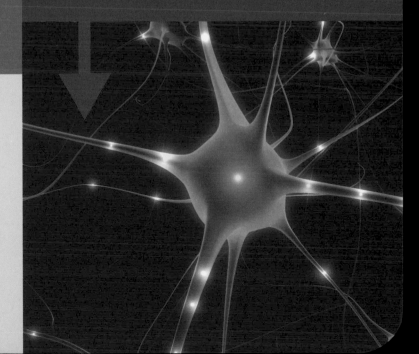

10 FACTS ABOUT WHAT GOES IN... AND WHAT COMES OUT

A human consumes as much food and drink in a lifetime as the weight of **one medium-sized blue whale.** #0338

If your **intestines** were stretched out, they would be more than four times as long as your body. #0339

You can eat upside down, as **special muscles** squeeze food toward your stomach. #0340

Eating snot can be good for you—it teaches your body to fight off germs. #0341

If you lose part of your **liver,** it can regrow itself. #0342

You can live without a **stomach.** #0343

Stomach acid is strong enough to dissolve metal. #0344

The average person **farts 14 times** a day. #0345

You have **billions of bacteria** living in your intestines. They help you digest food. #0346

Your stomach avoids **eating itself** by coating its own inside with thick mucus! #0347

Your brain is made up of **85% WATER**—the same as a **CABBAGE!** #0348

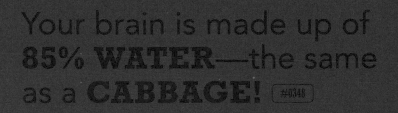

If you wear **headphones,** your ears make extra **earwax.** #0349

Your saliva (spit), tears, earwax, snot, and sweat all contain **chemicals that kill germs.** #0350

Most people sweat about **two teacups of liquid** per day, but it can be as much as a small bucketful! #0351

You can have a heart, lungs, kidney, liver, hand, or even face **TRANSPLANTED** from another person. #0352

Sometimes if a patient is given a **FAKE MEDICINE,** it can affect them like a real drug because they believe they will get better—it's called the "placebo effect." #0353

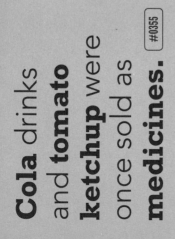

Before anesthetics, people having a limb amputated would **bite down on a piece of leather** to help deal with the pain. #0354

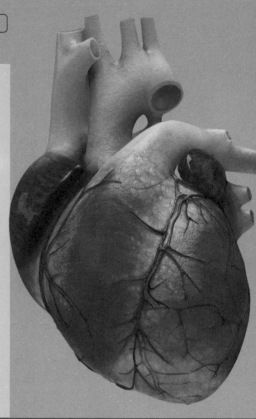

Cola drinks and **tomato ketchup** were once sold as **medicines.** #0355

medicine

10 FACTS ABOUT YOUR OUTSIDES

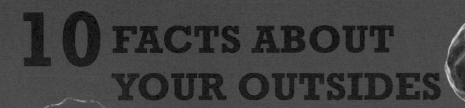

Every day, you shed about **40 million** dead skin cells. #0356

Dust is mainly dead skin cells. #0357

You have about **5 million hairs** on your body. #0358

Your skin is as heavy as wearing **four winter coats.** #0359

In a lifetime, you'll leave up to **44 pounds** of dead skin lying around. #0360

Fingernails and **toenails** grow faster in hot weather. #0361

Most people have tiny creepy-crawlies called **mites** living around their eyelashes. #0362

Your **nose gets runny** when you cry because tears from the eyes drain into the nose. #0363

Xie Qiuping of China holds the record for the longest hair in the world, at **18 feet.** #0364

Humans have been decorating their nails for more than **5,000 years.** #0365

10 AMAZING BODY NUMBERS

If all the **DNA** in your body was unraveled and stretched out, it could reach to the **Sun and back.** #0366

Frenchwoman Jeanne Calment lived to be **122 years old,** longer than anyone else on record. #0367

A Russian woman, Mrs. Vassilyev, is thought to have had **69 children**—32 twins, 21 triplets, and 16 quadruplets. #0368

Every human started off as **one cell,** for about the first half-hour that they existed. #0369

A sneeze zooms out of your nose and mouth at around **90 miles** per hour. #0370

Robert Wadlow, the **tallest person ever,** measured **8 feet 11 inches** and had **size 37 feet.** #0371

Lucia Zarate, the **smallest person ever**, was **20 inches** tall and weighed 4.6 pounds. #0372

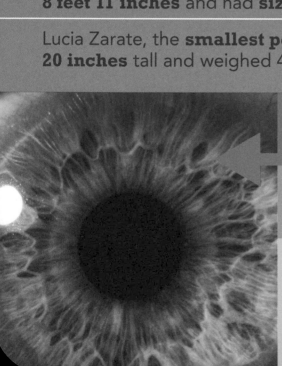

The **human eye** can see stars that are **millions of miles away.** #0373

Park Ranger **Roy Sullivan** survived being struck by lightning **seven times.** #0374

Charles Osborne of Iowa **hiccupped** nonstop for 68 years. #0375

Because you blink around

 **TIMES
A MINUTE...**

... you actually spend two years of your waking life with your **EYES SHUT.** #0376

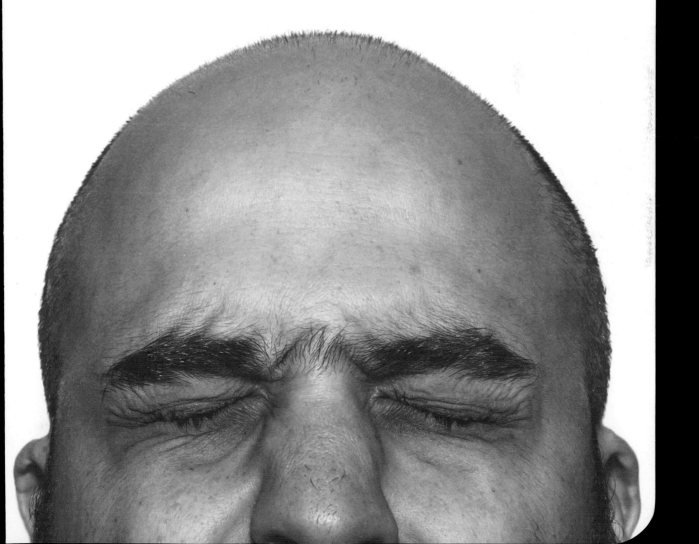

THE GREAT WALL OF CHINA was started around 500 BC and is over **13,000 MILES LONG.** That's as far as the distance from the North Pole to the South Pole! #0377

HISTORY YOU HAVE TO HEAR

Chapter 3

4 FACTS ON CHINA'S SECRET ARMY

Emperor **Qin Shi Huangdi** of China (259 BC–210 BC) wanted to **live forever,** so he built a huge burial mound to protect his body in the afterlife. #0378

At least **8,000 CLAY SOLDIERS** guard the tomb, as well as **130 CHARIOTS** and **670 HORSES.** #0379

The burial mound is believed to contain **booby traps to protect his body,** which is also surrounded by rivers of poisonous **mercury!** #0380

Every soldier's face was designed separately so **no two warriors look the same.** #0381

10 FACTS ABOUT THE WORLD'S BLOODIEST BATTLES

The world's **longest war** lasted for **116 years.** It was between England and France and started in 1337. #0382

The world's **shortest war** lasted just **38 minutes,** when a British fleet attacked the island of Zanzibar in 1896. #0383

Between **62 and 78 million** people died during World War II (1939–1945). #0384

During the Mongol conquests (1207–1472) **17% of the world's population died.** #0385

Nearly **2 million** German and Russian soldiers were **killed or wounded** during a battle at Stalingrad (1942–1943). #0386

During the Battle of the Somme, on July 1 1916, around **19,240 of the British army were killed.** #0387

Around **51,000** soldiers died in a **three-day battle** during the American Civil War (1861–1865). #0388

Confederate General "Stonewall" Jackson was mistakenly **killed by his own men.** #0389

The **largest naval battle** took place at Salamis in Greece about **2,500 years** ago. #0390

The **largest tank and aerial battles** happened at the same time, at Kursk in 1942, between Germans and Russians. #0391

5 EXPLORATORY FACTS ABOUT EXPLORERS

The Norwegian explorer **ROALD AMUNDSEN** was the first man to reach the **SOUTH POLE,** in 1911. #0392

During his lifetime, explorer **IBN BATTUTA** (1304–1368 or 1369) traveled 75,000 miles by foot, camel, and ship—as far as three times around the world. #0393

On an expedition in 1862, British explorer **JOHN SPEKE** became temporarily deaf after a **BEETLE** crawled into his ear and he tried to remove it with a knife! #0394

In 1860, **ROBERT BURKE** and **WILLIAM WILLS** walked across Australia in search of an **INLAND SEA.** They discovered there was no sea, but then died trying to get home. #0395

In 1642, Dutch explorer **ABEL TASMAN** sailed round the whole of **AUSTRALIA** without ever realizing it existed! #0396

Instead of using maps, **AUSTRALIAN ABORIGINALS** sang songs about landmarks such as rocks, trees, and waterholes to help them remember paths across the continent. #0391

4 FACTS ABOUT LOOOONG MARCHES

In 1846, the American **Mormon Battalion** marched over **1,860 miles** from Council Bluffs, Iowa, to San Diego, California. Their march helped the U.S. government to gain control of large areas of the American continent. `#0398`

From 1096, Christian soldiers marched and sailed out of **EUROPE** to the Holy Land in an attempt to rid it of Muslim control. Many thousands of people, including children, took part. `#0399`

In 334 BC, **ALEXANDER THE GREAT** led his army of around **50,000 MACEDONS** out of Europe into Asia on a journey that lasted until he died 11 years later. `#0400`

In 1812, Emperor **Napoleon** of France led his Grand Army of **685,000** men on a mission to invade Russia. It's estimated that there were only **70,000 survivors.** `#0401`

5 EMPIRE FACTS THAT TOTALLY RULE

The **LARGEST-EVER EMPIRE** in the world was the **BRITISH EMPIRE,** which peaked in 1922 when it covered over a fifth of the world's lands. #0402

The **ROMAN EMPIRE** included millions of people living over a large area, and they kept track of everyone by counting them! Just like our modern-day **CENSUS.** #0403

The empire that lasted the longest was the ancient empire of **CHINA**— for well over **2,000 YEARS!** #0404

Today, **JAPAN** is the only country in the world that calls itself an **EMPIRE** and has an emperor. #0405

At one time, European colonial empires and Chinese and Japanese empires controlled **EVERY MODERN-DAY COUNTRY IN THE WORLD** except Iran, Thailand, Afghanistan, Bhutan, and Liberia, which were never fully conquered. #0406

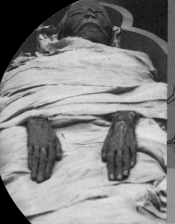

The **Great Pyramid** in Egypt was built in **2560 BC** and was originally 481 feet tall! #0407

The pyramid is made up of **2.3 million limestone blocks...** #0408

... and took 100,000 workers **20 years** to complete! #0409

The Egyptian **god of the dead** was called Anubis. He had the head of a jackal. #0410

The Egyptian **goddess of pregnancy and childbirth** was a hippopotamus called Taweret. #0411

Queen Hatshepsut of Egypt took the title of king. She dressed as a king, and even wore a false beard! #0412

Tutankhamun was only nine years old when he became pharaoh. #0413

Children in Ancient Egypt didn't wear much clothing, because it was so hot. #0414

When an Egyptian body was **mummified,** its brain was removed through one of its nostrils... #0415

... and the liver, intestines, lungs, and stomach were put in **canopic jars.** #0416

The **ANCIENT POLYNESIAN PEOPLES** had no navigation instruments, but sailed across big distances of open sea using only **THEIR SENSES!**

They would watch the stars, feel the motion of the waves, listen to wildlife, and follow weather signs. #0417

5 FACTS ABOUT VOTES FOR WOMEN

In 1718, a small group of female Swedish craftworkers were the **first women in the world** allowed to vote in elections. #0418

In 1756, Lydia Chapin Taft became the **first woman voter in North America** when she voted in Massachusetts Colony, then ruled by Britain. #0419

The first country to give all women the vote was **New Zealand, in 1893.** #0420

British women aged 30 and over got the vote in **1918,** while women in **Switzerland** had to wait until **1971.** #0421

Today, women are still unable to vote in **Saudi Arabia,** where they are also not permitted to drive a car. #0422

3 ARTY FACTS

The world's **oldest painting** is over **40,000 years old**—a red sphere of paint and handprints on a cave wall in El Castillo in Spain. #0423

One of the most **expensive paintings** in the world is "The Card Players" by Paul Cezanne, which sold in 2011 for **$250 million.** #0424

The oldest pieces of **pottery** in the world were found in 2012 by Chinese archaeologists. At **20,000 years old,** they were made at a time when much of the world was covered with ice! #0425

3 FACTS ABOUT WONDROUS WALLS

Hadrian's wall, a **75-mile wall,** was built for the Roman Emperor Hadrian to prevent attacks by raiders from the north of Britain. #0426

During the AD 770s, King **Offa of Mercia** in central England ordered a border to be dug to keep the Welsh out of his kingdom. The ditch is **66 feet wide** and can still be seen today. #0428

The **ancient wall** that stretches around Rome is **12 miles long, 53 feet tall,** and has **383 towers, 18 main gates—and 116 toilets!** #0427

10 FACTS ABOUT GODS AND EMPERORS

The Japanese believe that their emperor is a descendant of **Amaterasu,** the goddess of the Sun and the Universe. #0429

The current Japanese emperor, Akihito, is the **125th emperor of Japan.** #0430

The Chinese emperor was called the **"Son of Heaven."** #0431

In 331 BC, **Alexander the Great** decided that the Egyptian sky-god, Amun, was his real father! #0432

Napoleon Bonaparte became Emperor of France in 1804—yet he was not even born in France! #0433

Napoleon made his **three brothers kings** and his **sister a grand duchess.** #0434

The Roman emperor, **Caligula,** went mad and appointed his horse, Incitatus, a priest. #0435

Diocletian was the first Roman emperor ever to resign. He retired to a palace in Croatia and grew cabbages instead. #0436

After he died in 44 BC, **Julius Caesar** was officially recognized as a **god** by the Roman State. #0437

When **Ogedei Khan** of the Mongol empire died in AD 1241, the Mongol armies fighting in Western Europe had to go home to Asia to elect a new emperor. #0438

4 GOLDEN NUGGETS ABOUT ANCIENT GREECE

In the Greek state of **Sparta, boys** were taken from their mothers at seven years old and sent to boot camps, where they were brought up in packs and competed in mock fights. #0439

The Ancient Greeks invented the **THEATER,** building huge amphitheaters for plays. All the actors were men—even those playing women's parts! #0440

The Ancient Greeks worshipped **many gods,** including twelve main gods and goddesses who lived on Mount Olympus. #0441

At 20, the Spartans were given a **TOUGH FITNESS AND LEADERSHIP TEST** in order to join the military, and their duty didn't end until they were 60. #0442

98

5 FASCINATING VIKING FACTS

The name **"VIKING"** comes from a language called Old Norse and means **"A PIRATE RAID."** [#0443]

Viking **LONGBOATS** were cleverly designed to **FLOAT HIGH** in the water and **LAND ON BEACHES**—so the Vikings could jump out of the ship and join a raid quickly. [#0444]

Wealthy Viking warriors were **BURIED OR BURNED IN THEIR SHIPS,** which they believed would carry them into the next world. [#0445]

The word **"BERSERK"** comes from "Berserkers"— terrifying Viking warriors who wore wolf or bearskin and howled in battle like wild animals. [#0446]

Vikings believed in several gods, including **THOR,** the god of thunder. Our word **"THURSDAY"** is named after Thor ("Thor's Day"). [#0447]

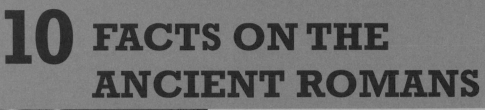

10 FACTS ON THE ANCIENT ROMANS

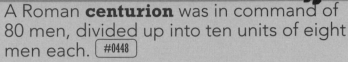

A Roman **centurion** was in command of 80 men, divided up into ten units of eight men each. #0448

The Romans discovered **concrete!** They mixed lime, volcanic ash, and water. #0449

Boys were **beaten** in Roman schools if they made mistakes! #0450

In Ancient Rome, urine was collected, and used for **tanning leather** and **cleaning togas.** #0451

The **Pantheon**, a temple to the gods, was built in AD 126. It is still the world's largest unreinforced concrete dome. #0452

Roman legions were named after their **qualities** or the **places** where they served. #0453

The Romans made **hamburgers** more than 2,000 years ago and ate **takeout food** from local bars. #0454

The world's **first fire engine** was invented by the engineer Hero, from Roman Egypt. #0455

The Romans heated their houses with the world's **first central heating system,** known as a hypocaust. #0456

While everyone else used scythes to cut corn, the Romans developed an early **combine harvester**! #0457

The Ancient Romans used guard dogs to guard their homes and, just like today, they even had **"BEWARE OF THE DOG"** signs. #0458

Some of the stones in the ancient circle of stones at **STONEHENGE** in southern England (constructed between 3100 and 1600 BC) weigh around  **29** tons.

They are over **16** feet tall. #0459

10 FACTS ON FIERCE FEMALE RULERS

In 1762, **Empress Catherine the Great** of Russia took the throne from her husband! #0460

The first woman to become a prime minister was **Sirimavo Bandaranaike,** who governed Sri Lanka during 1960–65, 1970–77 and 1994–2000. #0461

Queen Victoria of England ruled from 1837 for 63 years and 216 days! #0462

Many of Queen Victoria's **40 grandchildren** became kings and queens of other European countries. #0463

Margaret Thatcher was **Britain's first female prime minister,** and was nicknamed **"The Iron Lady"** because of her strong-willed leadership style. #0464

None of the 43 American presidents and numerous vice-presidents have been women. #0465

The first woman to become a president was **Isabel Peron,** who governed Argentina in 1974. #0466

In 2012, **Queen Elizabeth II** celebrated 60 years on the British throne. #0467

Women have ruled the Netherlands for **over 100 years!** #0468

Mary Queen of Scots was only six days old when she became Queen of Scotland in 1542. #0469

3 FACTS ABOUT THE INSPIRATIONAL INCAS

The Incas of South America could not read or write, so they used lengths of knotted, colored strings called **quipus** to keep records. #0470

The Incas built around **25,000 miles of roads**. Messengers ran along them day and night carrying messages for the emperor. #0471

The Incas cut and fitted together **stone bricks** so perfectly that their walls didn't need any mortar to hold them in place. #0472

10 FACTS ABOUT CRAZY RULERS

In 1258, the Mongol army attacked Baghdad and killed at least **200,000 of its 1 million people.**
#0473

When an Iranian city rebelled against his high taxes in the 1400s, Central Asian conqueror Timur **killed all 70,000 inhabitants.** #0474

The Aztecs of Central America **sacrificed humans to satisfy their gods!** #0475

In the 1500s, Russian ruler Ivan the Terrible **killed his own son** during an argument. #0476

Kaiser Wilhelm II of Germany abdicated in 1918 after almost **13 million soldiers** died during World War I between 1914 and 1918. #0477

During **Pol Pot's** rule of Cambodia, between 1975 and 1979, about **2 million** people were killed—a third of the population. #0478

In the 540s BC, **King Nabonidus of Babylon** ate **grass** and thought he was a **goat!** #0479

When feared dictator **Joseph Stalin** had a stroke in 1953, his ministers and police were too scared to call a doctor for him! #0480

Idi Amin, president of Uganda from 1971 to 1979, killed up to 500,000 opponents. #0481

In 1976, **President Jean-Bédel Bokassa,** military ruler of the Central African Republic, declared himself **emperor!** #0482

3 FACTS ABOUT SAILING THE SEVEN SEAS

Between 1676 and 1710, **William Dampier** from England completed **three round-the-world voyages**—one time as a pirate, raiding enemy ships! #0483

In 1895, **Joshua Slocum** set out to become the first man to **sail around the world by himself,** though he did stop many times along the route. #0484

The first man to sail alone around the world without stopping was **Englishman Robin Knox-Johnston,** who did it in 313 days in 1968–69. The current record is 45 days and 13 hours. #0485

4 ANCIENT FACTS ABOUT CIVILIZATIONS

Writing **words** using pictures and signs first appeared about **5,500 years ago.** It was another 2,000 years before the first alphabet appeared. #0486

The world's oldest known scientific **CALCULATOR** was made around **100 BC.** #0487

Around 2110 BC, King Ur-Nammu of Ur became the first ruler to **WRITE DOWN THE LAWS OF HIS LAND** in a written code. There were 57 laws. #0488

Around 500 BC, King Darius, ruler of the Persian Empire, built a **royal road** to a capital city over **1,500 miles away.** On foot, the journey would take at least 90 days. #0489

10 STAR-SPANGLED FACTS ABOUT THE U.S.

The U.S. was **declared independent from Britain** on July 4, 1776. #0490

Up to 19 presidents have had **attempts on their lives** while in office, and four have died **natural deaths.** #0491

The American national anthem is called **"The Star Spangled Banner."** #0492

Due to unusual circumstances, two **unelected men** were running the U.S. between 1974 and 1976. #0493

The term **"First Lady"** for a president's wife comes from President Zachary Taylor in 1849, when he used it for his late wife at her funeral. #0494

Four U.S. presidents—Lincoln, Garfield, McKinley, and Kennedy—were **assassinated**. #0495

Eight of the first nine **presidents** were British, because they were born before the country became independent! #0496

The government met in eight different cities before settling on **Washington D.C.** as the U.S. capital in 1790. #0497

Before joining the U.S., the states of **Vermont, Texas, and Hawaii** were all independent republics with their own governments. #0498

Grover Cleveland is the only president to serve **two non-consecutive terms,** so he is both the 22nd and the 24th president. #0499

The **NAZCA** people of South America cut **HUNDREDS OF SHAPES** of animals, birds, trees, and flowers into the desert between AD 400 and 650, some as big as 880 feet across.

Since they didn't have airplanes, they would **NEVER HAVE KNOWN** what they really looked like. #0500

As of December 2011, **CHINA** is the **MOST POPULATED COUNTRY IN THE WORLD,** with almost **20%** of the world's entire population. #0501

SOCIETY AND CULTURE SHOCKERS

Chapter 4

3 MOMENTOUS MILITARY FACTS

Nine countries in the world have **nuclear weapons.** #0502

15 countries, including Costa Rica, have **no military forces at all.** #0503

There are about **1.4 million** men and women on active duty in the **U.S. military** and roughly the same in the reserves. #0504

5 COUNTRY NUMBER-CRUNCHERS

RUSSIA is the world's **LARGEST COUNTRY,** covering over 6.6 million square miles. That's 13% of the world's land area. #0505

The world's **SMALLEST COUNTRY** is the **VATICAN CITY** in Rome. It covers just 0.16 square miles or around 62 soccer fields. #0506

At their tallest point, the coral islands of the Maldives in the Indian Ocean peek out of the sea at a maximum height of **JUST 8 FEET.** #0507

Tibet is the highest region in the world, towering above sea level at a height of **16,076 FEET.** #0508

The border between Canada and the United States is the **LONGEST INTERNATIONAL BORDER IN THE WORLD** between two countries at **5,525 MILES.** #0509

The world's longest tunnel is the Thirlmere Aqueduct, a 96-mile water tunnel under the north of England.

10 POPULAR FACTS ABOUT POPULATIONS

The world's **population** is over **7 billion** and rising fast. #0511

In **1960,** the population of the world was **3 billion** people. #0512

During 2011, about **135 million** people were born in the world... #0513

... and **57 million** died. That's an increase of 78 million people in just one year. #0514

The world's population is increasing by **2.4 people a second.** #0520

252 babies are born in the world every minute, or **4.2 births a second.** #0519

107 people die in the world every minute, or **1.8 deaths a second**. #0515

The highest life expectancy in the world is in Japan— **83 years.** #0518

More than **60%** of the world's population live in **Asia.** #0517

On May 29, 2007, for the first time in human history, more people lived in **cities and towns** than in the countryside! #0516

4 FACTS GOING CRAZY FOR COUNTRIES

Most of the countries in the world have a coastline, but 48 are **landlocked,** which means their citizens have to pass through another country to get to the sea. #0521

Nearly **47,000 PEOPLE** pack into every square mile of the **PRINCIPALITY OF MONACO,** making it the most densely populated country in the world. #0522

There are only **4.4 people** for every square mile of **Mongolia,** the world's emptiest country. #0523

Japan has the oldest population in the world, with nearly a quarter of people aged **OVER 65.** #0524

In 2012, the **TALLEST BUILDING IN THE WORLD** was the **BURJ KHALIFA** skyscraper in Dubai, which towers at nearly 2,725 feet—that's well over

100

stacked houses! #0525

10 TONGUE-TWISTING FACTS ON LANGUAGES

The most commonly spoken language in the world is **Mandarin Chinese,** spoken by **845 million people.** #0526

The United Nations recognizes **six official world languages:** Mandarin Chinese, Spanish, English, Arabic, Russian, and French. #0527

Around the world, people speak about **6,500 different languages.** #0528

Approximately 83 of these are spoken by **80% of the world's population**. #0529

Approximately 473 of the world's languages are **almost extinct** and spoken only by a few people. #0530

Approximately one language dies out in the world **every two weeks,** when its last speaker dies. #0531

The **Sumerian language** of the Middle East is one of the earliest on record, dating back to around **2900 BC**. #0532

Most **European languages** are closely related to each other, such as German and Dutch. #0533

However, **Euskara,** the language of the Basque people in northern Spain, is **unrelated to any other known language** in the world. #0534

In 1825, blind Frenchman **Louis Braille** developed a language that could be read by blind people by feeling a series of bumps on paper. #0535

3 BOREDOM-BUSTING BOOK FACTS

The world's **longest novel** is Marcel Proust's *A la recherche du temps perdu* (In Search of Lost Time), which has more than **1.5 million words** and was originally published in seven volumes. #0536

The **oldest printed book** is the Diamond Sutra, a Buddhist religious text printed in China in AD 868. #0537

In 1969, the French writer Georges Perec wrote *La Disparition* (The Void) **without using the letter "e."** He followed that up in 1972 with *Les Revenentes* (The Ghosts) in which **"e" is the only vowel used.** #0538

DISABLED ATHLETES have a long history of competing in the **OLYMPIC GAMES.** An American gymnast competed in 1904 with one leg, and a one-armed Hungarian took part in the shooting events in 1948 and 1952.

#0539

5 FACTS TO MAKE MONEY TALK

The **POUND STERLING** used in the U.K. is the **WORLD'S OLDEST CURRENCY** still in use. The silver penny was first introduced around **1,300 YEARS AGO,** and 240 silver pennies weighed one pound (£1). #0540

It is believed that the first coins were produced in Aegina in Greece in around **700 BC.** #0541

PAPER MONEY was first used in China in 1024, but we don't know what it looked like since none has survived. #0542

In 1946, the **HUNGARIAN NATIONAL BANK** issued a banknote for **100 QUINTILLION PENGO** (100 million million million pengo). #0543

Somalia once issued a **COIN** in the shape of a **GUITAR!** #0544

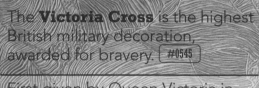

The **Victoria Cross** is the highest British military decoration, awarded for bravery. [#0545]

First given by Queen Victoria in 1857, the Victoria Cross has been awarded **1,357 times.** [#0546]

The **Purple Heart** is awarded to U.S. servicemen or women wounded or killed in service. [#0547]

U.S. presidents have awarded almost **2 million** Purple Hearts. [#0548]

The **Freedom Award** from the International Rescue Committee is for extraordinary contributions to the cause of refugees and human freedom. [#0549]

The **Turner Prize** is an annual visual arts prize in the U.K. In 1999, Tracy Emin's controversial shortlisted piece featured an unmade, messy bed! [#0550]

The highest award in Denmark is called the **Order of the Elephant,** usually given to heads of state and members of the royal family. [#0551]

The **"British Order of the Bath"** gets its name from the old ceremony of ritually bathing a new knight to purify him. [#0552]

Swedish inventor **Alfred Nobel** left money in his will for international prizes for peace, chemistry, physics, medicine, economics, and literature. [#0553]

Nobel Prizes bring prestige for winners—and a small fortune! In 2012, each prize was worth around **$1.2 million.** [#0554]

3 FASCINATING FACTS ABOUT WORLD RELIGIONS

There are around **2.5 billion Christians** in the world today, around one third of the world's population, making Christianity the most popular religion in the world. #0555

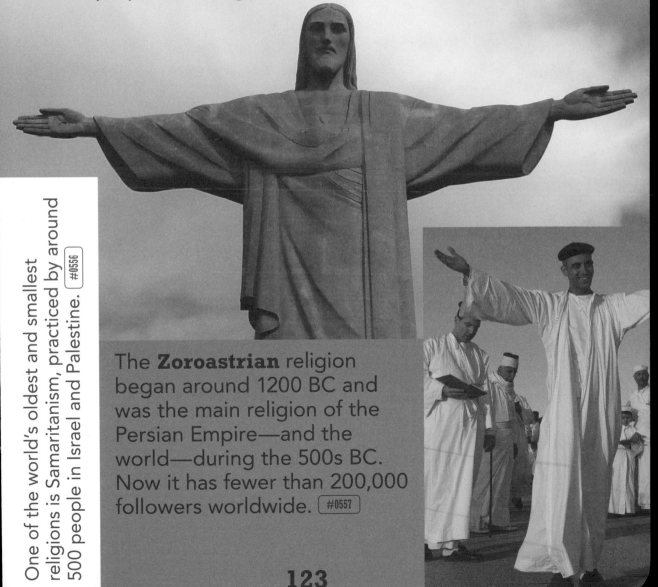

One of the world's oldest and smallest religions is Samaritanism, practiced by around 500 people in Israel and Palestine. #0556

The **Zoroastrian** religion began around 1200 BC and was the main religion of the Persian Empire—and the world—during the 500s BC. Now it has fewer than 200,000 followers worldwide. #0557

More copies of the **BIBLE** are **SHOPLIFTED** than of any other book. #0558

10 MIND-BENDING FACTS ABOUT GOVERNMENTS

Elizabeth II of the U.K. is also queen of **16 Commonwealth countries,** including Canada, Australia, New Zealand, and Jamaica. #0559

The current **longest-serving head of state**, King Rama IX of Thailand, has been in power since 1946. #0560

The current **oldest head of state** is Cuthbert Sebastian, who was born in 1921. #0561

No king or queen has entered the **U.K. House of Commons** since 1642... #0562

... when Charles I stormed in with his soldiers and **tried to arrest** five members of Parliament. #0563

Of all the countries in the world, 44 are monarchies, including 16 Commonwealth nations. #0564

The **biggest democracy** in the world is India. **714 million people** were eligible to vote in the Indian general election of 2009. #0565

A **theocracy** is a system of government based on religion—the head of state is selected by a religious group. #0566

There are two theocracies—the **Vatican City** in Rome, home of the Roman Catholic Church, and **Iran,** an Islamic republic. #0567

In **Australia** it is compulsory for citizens over the age of 18 to vote. #0568

5 FLAG-WAVING FACTS

The world's **FIRST FLAGS** were used in ancient China to represent different parts of the army. #0569

The **ROMAN CAVALRY** carried a square flag known as a **VEXILLUM,** from which we get the term vexillology—the study of flags. #0570

The **OLDEST NATIONAL FLAG** in use is Denmark's white cross on a red background, which is nearly 800 years old. #0571

There is no significance to the **12 YELLOW STARS** that appear on the blue **EUROPEAN UNION** flag— the stars just make a neat circle! #0572

The **UNION FLAG OF THE UK** also appears on **29** other national, provincial, state, and territory flags around the world, including the Australian national flag. #0573

4 CURIOUS FACTS ABOUT CITIES

14 countries, including Chile, Bolivia, and the Netherlands, have **two capital cities.** One state, South Africa, has **three** capitals! `#0574`

16 COUNTRIES have capital cities with the same or very similar name, including Kuwait (Kuwait), Mexico (Mexico City), Brazil (Brasilia), and Tunisia (Tunis). `#0575`

The **highest capital city** in the world is **La Paz,** the administrative capital of Bolivia in South America. It stands 11,940 feet above sea level. `#0576`

At the moment, **Shanghai** in China is the world's most populated city proper, with over 17 million people. `#0577`

Havergal Brian's Symphony No. 1, the Gothic Symphony, is the **LARGEST ORCHESTRAL PIECE OF MUSIC** ever written. It needs:

32 wind players,

52 brass players,

82 string players,

4 keyboard players,

24 percussionists,

a choir of at least 600, a children's choir of 100, and four soloists. #0578

128

10 TOE-TAPPING MUSICAL FACTS

The **bestselling pop single** of all time is "White Christmas," released by Bing Crosby in 1942. #0579

The **bestselling album** of all time is "Thriller," released by Michael Jackson in 1982. #0580

In May 2009, more than 100,000 Hindus formed the **biggest choir ever** assembled, in Hyderabad, India. #0581

The **saxophone** is named after its inventor, Adolphe Sax, and the **sousaphone** is named after the American composer John Philip Sousa. #0582

The earliest evidence for the existence of **bagpipes** is in ancient engravings dating back to **1300 BC.** #0583

Wolfgang Amadeus Mozart, born in Austria in 1756, started composing at just **five years old!** #0584

Bagpipes arrived in Scotland in the 1300s and developed into the highland pipes we recognize today. #0585

On the U.S. Billboard chart, the **Beatles** hold the record for **the most Number One hit singles at 20.** #0586

John Cage composed 4'33" in 1952. Instruments play **no notes at all** during its four-minute, 33-second length! #0587

George Beauchamp designed the **first electric guitar** prototype in 1931. It was nicknamed the "Frying Pan" because of its shape! #0588

Some people around the world have rather **UNUSUAL** beauty rituals, including teeth sharpening,

ear elongations,

nose studs,

lip plates,

or even giraffe necks! #0589

4 SENSATIONAL FACTS ABOUT THE CENT

There are **150 BILLION U.S. 1 CENT COINS** in circulation. #0590

If they were piled up on each other, they would stand **144,469 miles high,** which is three-fifths of the way to the Moon. #0591

Count one of these coins every second and it would take you **4,757 YEARS** to complete counting. #0592

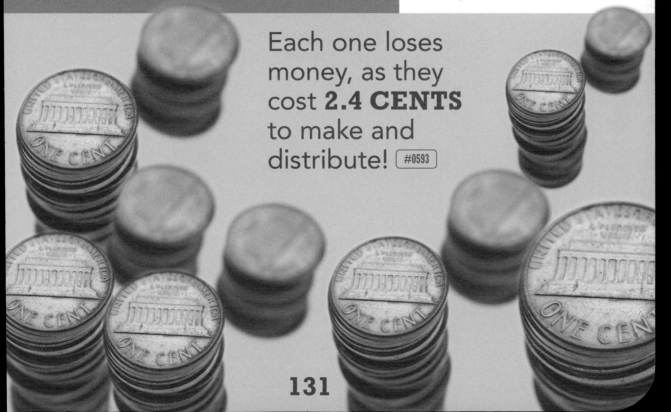

Each one loses money, as they cost **2.4 CENTS** to make and distribute! #0593

10 LUDICROUS FACTS ABOUT LAWS

In the U.K., it's an **act of treason** to place a postage stamp of the Queen's head upside down. #0594

In France, it is forbidden to call a pig **Napoleon.** #0595

In Singapore, **chewing gum** is banned. #0596

In Florida, it is illegal to **skateboard** in a police station. #0597

In the U.K., the head of any **dead whale** found on the coast is legally the property of the king; the tail belongs to the queen. #0598

In London, England, it is illegal to **flag down a taxi** if you have the **plague.** #0599

In Alabama, it's illegal to be **blindfolded** while driving a vehicle. #0600

In Eraclea in Italy, it is forbidden to build **sandcastles.** #601

In Vermont, women must obtain written permission from their husbands to wear **false teeth.** #0602

In Switzerland, it's illegal to **flush a toilet** in an apartment after 10pm. #0603

3 FACTS ABOUT EYE-POPPING PRICES

The world's most expensive camera sold for a record-breaking **$2.8 million!** It was one of only 25 made in 1923. #0604

Napoleon Bonaparte's sword is one of the top selling antiques on record. It sold for over **$6 million.** #0605

In 1969, the actor Richard Burton paid **$1.1 million** for a pear-shaped diamond to give to his wife, Elizabeth Taylor. It has since been resold for about **$5 million.**
#0606

4 WONDERFUL FACTS ON WORLD ORGANIZATIONS

The world's oldest international organization was set up in Britain in 1839 to campaign for the abolition of slavery. Still running today, it's now called **Anti-Slavery International.** `#0607`

Recognizing that humankind could not afford a third world war, the **UNITED NATIONS** was formed in 1945 to promote world peace. It has 193 members. `#0608`

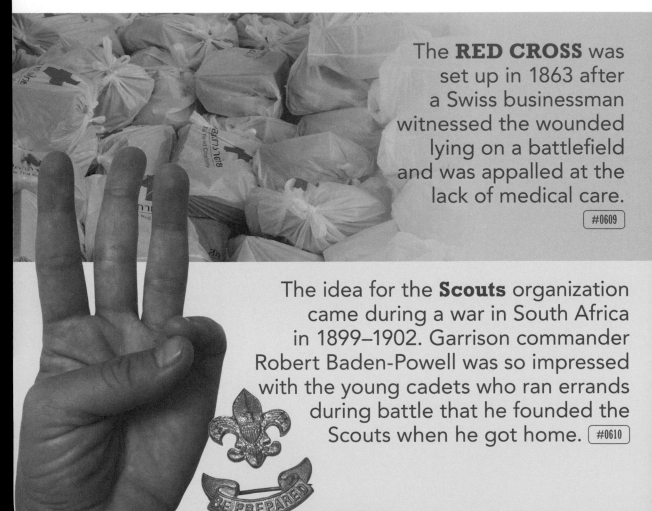

The **RED CROSS** was set up in 1863 after a Swiss businessman witnessed the wounded lying on a battlefield and was appalled at the lack of medical care. `#0609`

The idea for the **Scouts** organization came during a war in South Africa in 1899–1902. Garrison commander Robert Baden-Powell was so impressed with the young cadets who ran errands during battle that he founded the Scouts when he got home. `#0610`

5 FREAKY FILM FACTS

The Academy Award **OSCAR** statue is modeled on a real person—Mexican film director and actor **EMILIO FERNÁNDEZ.** #0611

JAMES CAMERON has directed the two highest earning movies of all time—*Avatar* and *Titanic*. Combined, they have made over $3.2 billion at the box office. #0612

If the figures for the highest earning film were to allow for price rises since release, *GONE WITH THE WIND* from 1939 would be the most successful. #0613

The **LONGEST FILM** ever made is the Danish experimental film *Modern Times Forever* (Stora Enso Building, Helsinki), which runs for **10 DAYS!** #0614

The first feature film with **DIALOGUE AND MUSIC** was *The Jazz Singer*, a musical released in 1927. #0615

10 SPORTING FACTS TO EXERCISE YOUR BRAIN

The **oldest sporting event** is the Newmarket Town Plate horse race, run almost every year in the U.K. since 1665. #0616

The **most popular sport** is soccer. Around 3.3 billion people watch or play the game. #0617

The **biggest ever soccer crowd** of nearly 200,000 fans watched the World Cup final between Brazil and Uruguay in Rio de Janeiro in 1950. #0618

The World Cup soccer competition has been held **19 times** since it started in 1930. #0619

More than **2 million people** lined the streets of Madrid to welcome home the winning Spanish World Cup soccer team in 2010. #0620

Around **15 million people** watch the Tour de France cycle race each year. #0621

Up to **400,000 people** watch the annual Indianapolis 500 motor race in the U.S.A. #0622

Formula 1 racing cars can reach speeds of up to **217 miles per hour!** #0623

In 1661, the **first yacht race** took place on the River Thames between King Charles II and his brother, the Duke of York. #0624

Ever since 2000, competitors have taken part in the annual **Mobile Phone Throwing** World Championship! #0625

In **TIBET,** it is considered **POLITE** to **STICK OUT YOUR TONGUE** at your guests. Imagine if you tried that at home! #0626

Chapter 5

THE WONDERS OF PLANET EARTH

In 1883, the eruption of a **VOLCANO** in Indonesia produced the **WORLD'S LOUDEST-EVER BANG,** which was heard in Australia, 3,000 miles away. #0627

Steamboat Geyser in Wyoming shoots jets of scalding water

In 1975, a cricket umpire was struck by lightning that **fused an iron joint** in his leg. #0629

300 feet into the air. #0628

The springs of Beppu, Japan, are so hot that people have used them to **boil eggs!** #0630

10 LAVA-LICIOUS FACTS ABOUT VOLCANOES

In 1815, the eruption of **Mount Tambora** in Indonesia spread an ash cloud around the world. #0631

Llullaillaco in the Atacama Desert is the **tallest active volcano in the world,** at 13,681 feet! #0632

In 1943, a new volcano in Mexico reached **five stories high in a week**—Mount Paricutin is now over 9,000 feet tall. #0633

The eruption of **Vesuvius** in Italy in AD 79 perfectly preserved the Roman city of Pompeii under a layer of ash—it lay buried for 1,700 years. #0634

Red-hot **lava** flows like sticky liquid. #0635

An eruption on the Caribbean island of Martinique in 1902 killed **almost everyone in the island's capital**— only a few survived. #0637

Over 60% of all volcanoes erupt **under water.** #0636

Mauna Loa on Hawaii has erupted roughly **every six years since** 1000 BC. #0638

In 1985, an eruption in South America buried the town of Armero under **16 feet of mud.** #0639

In 1952, a Japanese ship, the *Kaiyo Maru,* sank when an **undersea volcano** erupted just below it. #0640

4 INTERESTING ISLAND FACTS

The volcanic island of Surtsey rose from the Atlantic Ocean in 1963, making it the **world's youngest island.** `#0641`

The **WORLD'S MOST REMOTE ISLAND,** Bouvet Island, is 930 miles from the nearest landmass, Antarctica. It would take a speedboat traveling at top speed nearly a day to reach it from Antarctica. `#0642`

The **world's smallest island** is Bishop Rock off the coast of Cornwall, England—it's just a rock with a lighthouse! `#0644`

Greenland is the **WORLD'S LARGEST ISLAND.** Australia is three times larger, but it is considered a continent. `#0643`

5 MASSIVE FACTS ABOUT MOUNTAINS

Mount Everest is the **WORLD'S HIGHEST MOUNTAIN** but Mauna Kea, Hawaii, rises higher from the ocean floor. #0645

The Himalayas contains all of the world's highest mountains, including **100 PEAKS OVER 22,950 FEET TALL.** They are still rising by 0.25 inches a year. #0646

Over **4,000 PEOPLE** have stood on the summit of Everest since the mountain was conquered in 1953. #0647

However, over **200 PEOPLE** have died trying to climb Everest. #0648

When Mount St. Helens blew its top in 1980, the volcano lost **1,300 FEET** from its height. #0649

In 1940, a tornado disturbed a hoard of **BURIED TREASURE,** raining gold coins on a Russian town. #0650

4 COOL FACTS ABOUT THE COAST

The Hawaiian island of Molokai has the **world's highest sea cliffs,** plunging 3,314 feet into the sea—the height of 22 Statue of Libertys. #0651

In 1999, a U.S. lighthouse was **moved 0.5 miles inland** to save it from toppling into the sea. #0653

The **GREAT BARRIER REEF** runs for **1,600 MILES** off eastern Australia and is so huge it can be seen from space. #0652

If all the world's coastlines were joined up, they would stretch over **528,000 MILES.** It would take a speedboat racing at top speed over a year to cruise past. #0654

The Atlantic Ocean is getting **1.5 inches wider each year!** #0655

The Mariana Trench in the Pacific is **Earth's deepest point**— so deep, it could submerge Mount Everest. #0656

The Pacific is Earth's deepest ocean, with an average depth of **13,780 feet.** #0657

The Pacific Ocean has more than **25,000 islands.** #0658

Seawater freezes at a **lower temperature** than fresh water, at 28.6°F. #0659

In 1933, a U.S. Navy ship caught in a Pacific storm survived a **112-foot high wave**—the biggest wave at sea ever recorded. #0660

The world's **longest mountain range** is called the mid-ocean ridge—it spans 7,022 miles around the globe. #0661

The water in a wave doesn't travel forward like you might think, it goes **around in a circle.** #0662

If you could remove all the **salt** from the oceans, it would cover Earth's dry land to a depth of **5 feet.** #0663

In 1900, 6,000 people died when the town of **Galveston, Texas,** was swamped by waves. #0664

The **Amazon River** carries more water than the next eight biggest rivers combined. #0665

The Iguazu Falls in South America consists of **275 waterfalls** along 1.7 miles of the Iguazu River. #0667

Lake Nyos in West Africa, which lies in the crater of an inactive volcano, once released a cloud of **poisonous volcanic gas** that killed 1,700 people. #0666

In Alaska, in 1964, **BUILDINGS SANK INTO THE GROUND** when an earthquake caused solid ground to turn to **LIQUID MUD.** #0668

The **world's deadliest earthquake** hit central China in 1556, killing 830,000 people. #0669

Nine out of ten earthquakes strike around the shores of the Pacific Ocean. #0670

Tsunamis (giant waves set off by earthquakes) can race across the ocean at **370 miles** per hour. #0671

In 1755, the Portuguese city of **Lisbon** was totally destroyed by an earthquake, fire, and tidal waves. #0672

In 1896, Japanese sailors out at sea hardly noticed a tsunami that went on to kill **28,000 people** on land. #0673

The Indonesian earthquake of 2004 released **more energy** than all the earthquakes in the previous five years combined. #0674

Often, before a tsunami strikes, all the **water drains away** from the shore, exposing the seabed. #0675

An earthquake in 1812 was so strong, it caused the Mississippi River to **flow backward.** #0676

In 1985, a **healthy baby** was found in a ruined hospital in Mexico City seven days after an earthquake destroyed the city. #0677

In 1976, scientists noticed animals behaving oddly in a Chinese city. The city was **evacuated** and two hours later an earthquake struck. #0678

4 CLEVER CAVE FACTS

Krubera Cave in Georgia, western Asia, is the **deepest known cave,** plunging deeper than 6,500 feet. It would take you about 30 seconds to fall that far! #0679

Stalactites are rocky needles hanging from cave ceilings, formed by dripping water. The **WORLD'S LONGEST STALACTITE** is 9 yards long in The White Chamber in Lebanon. #0680

Mammoth Cave in Kentucky is the **WORLD'S LARGEST CAVE SYSTEM,** with over 390 miles of linked caves and passages. #0681

The **longest underwater cave** found so far is a **134-mile maze** of flooded passages in Mexico. It's not yet been fully explored. #0682

5 WINDING FACTS ABOUT RIVERS

The area of land that contributes water to a river is called a "basin." The basin of the Amazon River covers **NEARLY HALF OF SOUTH AMERICA!** #0683

The Amazon empties so much water into the Atlantic that fresh water can be found **112 MILES OUT TO SEA.** #0684

A huge underground river runs under the **NILE,** containing **SIX TIMES MORE WATER** than the Nile itself. #0685

The **WORLD'S SHORTEST RIVER** is the Roe River in Montana, which is only 68 yards long—half the length of a soccer field. #0686

The Yellow River in China is the **WORLD'S MUDDIEST RIVER,** dumping over a billion tons of silt into the sea each year. #0687

Hurricanes are huge spinning storms with winds of over **75 miles per hour!** #0688

Tornadoes are much smaller than hurricanes, but with winds **three times as strong.** #0689

Hurricanes spin **clockwise** south of the Equator and **counterclockwise** north of the Equator. #0690

A tornado in Italy sucked a **baby** out of his carriage, carried him **98 yards,** and set him down safely. #0691

A tornado in England plucked all of the **feathers** off hens in a coop. #0692

Waterspouts whipped up by hurricanes at sea can tower over **300 feet.** #0693

In 1928, a hurricane dumped over **2.5 billion tons of seawater** on the Caribbean island of Puerto Rico. #0694

In 1992, a hurricane shifted a **whole island** closer to the U.S. coast! #0695

A hurricane unleashes the same amount of energy as a **nuclear bomb.** #0696

A U.S. tornado lifted a **train off the tracks** and dumped it **27 yards** away. #0697

Six thousand years ago, the **SAHARA DESERT** was lush and leafy, enjoyed by the hippos, giraffes, and elephants that lived there. #0698

5 ELECTRIFYING THUNDER AND LIGHTNING FACTS

A bolt of lightning heats the air around it to **16,650°F**—five times hotter than the surface of the Sun. #0699

Lightning travels downward at **930 MILES PER HOUR** and even faster upward. #0700

Right now, there are about **2,000 THUNDERSTORMS** raging around the world. #0701

Lightning is very dangerous—it **KILLS AND INJURES** more people each year than hurricanes or tornadoes. #0702

People in the town of Tororo in East Africa hear thunder about **250 DAYS A YEAR.** #0703

The temperature rises around **118°F** **FOR EVERY MILE** you travel toward the center of Earth. #0704

Vast **underground lakes** lie beneath some of Earth's greatest deserts, including the Sahara. Some of the water is being tapped for farming and cities. #0705

At the center of a raging hurricane is a calm area called the **eye,** where there is very little wind. #0706

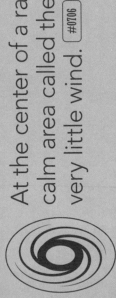

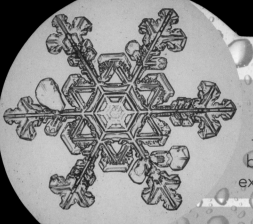

All snowflakes have **six sides** but no two that have ever been studied are exactly alike. #0707

In 1881, a violent storm rained **crabs and sea snails** on an English town over 37 miles from the coast. #0708

In 1934, a **231-mile-per-hour** gust of wind was recorded at Mount Washington! #0709

Snowflakes measuring **15 inches,** larger than dinner plates, have fallen in Montana. #0710

In 1986, hailstones the size of **grapefruits** fell on a town in Bangladesh, killing 92 people. #0711

If all the moisture in the air fell as rain, it would cover Earth's surface to a depth of **1 inch.** #0712

The town of Calama in the Atacama Desert had had no rain for **400 years,** until a shower in 1972. #0713

By the time you've read this sentence, over **900 million tons of rain** will have fallen around Earth. #0714

In 1882, two **frozen frogs** were found inside hailstones in Iowa. #0715

Commonwealth Bay in Antarctica occasionally experiences winds of **200 miles per hour.** #0716

The Earth acts like a **GIANT MAGNET** because of its core of molten metal. That's why compasses point north. #0717

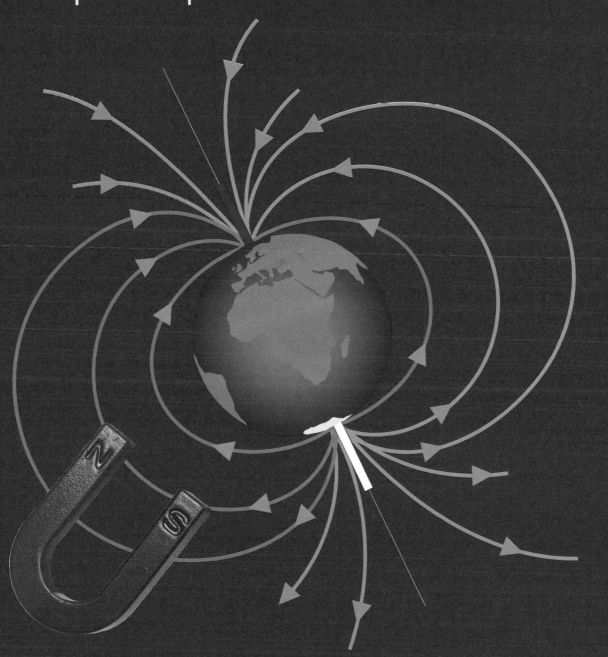

The **world's largest swamp,** the Pantanal in Brazil, covers an area larger than Pennsylvania. #0718

The vast **Ganges Delta** in Asia, a swampy area where two mighty rivers meet, covers an area the size of Virginia. #0719

The **Great Rift Valley** is a **3,700-mile trench** that has been created where two of the giant plates that make up Earth's crust are pulling apart. #0720

Earth's **deepest mine** is TauTona Goldmine in South Africa, 4,265 feet deep. #0721

The **deepest hole ever bored**, Kola Borehole in Russia, descends 13,342 feet! #0722

All of the gold mined in a year would fit inside the **average living room.** #0723

The **largest gold nugget** ever found is the "Welcome Stranger," found in 1869 in Australia. #0724

The **first diamond found in South Africa** was picked up by children on a beach. #0725

The world's **largest diamond,** the Cullinan Diamond, was the size of a large egg. #0726

The **world's most valuable gem** is painite, a small crystal found only in Burma. #0727

Earth's oldest fossils are 3.4 billion years old. #0728

The **world's largest pearl,** the Pearl of Lao Tzu, is about the same size as a basketball. #0729

Only **one in a thousand oysters** contains a **pearl.** #0730

5 DRAMATIC FACTS ABOUT DESERTS

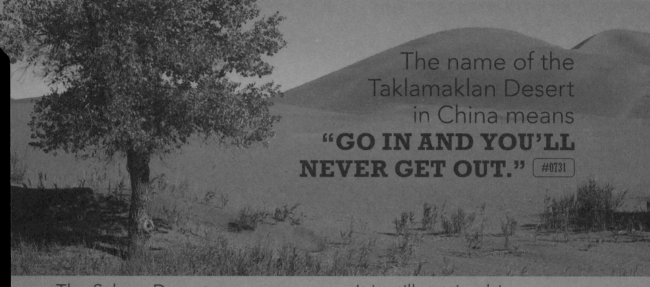

The name of the Taklamaklan Desert in China means **"GO IN AND YOU'LL NEVER GET OUT."** #0731

The Sahara Desert, **EARTH'S BIGGEST DESERT,** covers an area about the size of the United States. #0732

It is still getting bigger—growing **30 MILES** south every year. #0733

Despite being covered in ice, **ANTARCTICA** is actually classed as a desert because it hardly ever snows! #0734

In 1913, the temperature at Furnace Creek in Death Valley, California, hit a sizzling **133°F**—the highest on record in the country. #0735

4 EARTH-SHATTERING EARTHQUAKE AND AVALANCHE FACTS

In 1970, an **earthquake** in Peru triggered an avalanche that buried the town of Yungay and its 20,000 inhabitants. #0736

A cliff collapse in northern England in 1993 sent a **HOTEL TUMBLING INTO THE SEA.** #0737

The cliffs of Holderness in Britain are moving **3 TO 6 FEET INLAND** each year as they are eaten away by the sea. #0738

In 1916, **avalanches** in the Alps killed 10,000 soldiers fighting in World War I. #0739

10 SPARKLING ICE FACTS

Antarctica holds **70% of Earth's fresh water,** locked up in ice. [#0740]

The largest iceberg ever seen was the size of **Jamaica!** It broke off Antarctica. [#0741]

The **tallest iceberg** ever spotted was a 548-foot whopper floating off Greenland. [#0742]

The Sahara Desert was covered by **glaciers** 450 million years ago. [#0743]

In 1991, the **5,000-year-old** preserved body of a huntsman was found in a glacier in the Alps. [#0744]

In 1848, ice blocked **Niagara Falls** for nearly two days, so people explored the dry riverbed. [#0745]

In 1912, 1,502 people died in icy waters when an **iceberg** sank the "unsinkable" ship, *Titanic.* [#0746]

In 1829, a chunk of ice weighing 4.5 pounds **inexplicably fell** on the town of Cordoba in Spain. [#0747]

If all the ice in Antarctica melted, sea levels would rise by **220 feet!** [#0748]

The South Pole is covered by a sheet of ice **8,858 feet** thick. [#0749]

In 1859, a shower of fish fell on Glamorgan, in Wales, when a strong updraft of wind sucked them out of the sea and dropped them inland. #0750

Chapter 6

SCIENCE AND
TECHNOLOGY
BRAINBUSTERS

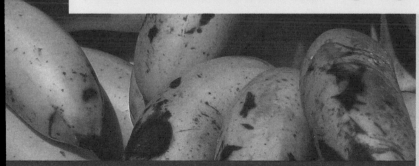

Humans share about
HALF OF THEIR DNA
with a banana. #0751

3 SHOCKING ELECTRICITY FACTS

Electricity travels as fast as the **speed of light**—about 186,000 miles per second. [#0752]

One 60-watt light bulb is the equivalent of about **25,000 fireflies.** [#0753]

An **electric eel** can produce an electric shock of 500 volts at one amp, enough to **kill an adult human.** [#0754]

5 PLANT BIOLOGY FACTS TO GROW YOUR MIND

Gregor Mendel, a scentist in the 1800s, came up with some of the first ideas on genetics (how traits are passed from one generation to the next) by looking at **PEA PODS AND THEIR FLOWERS.** #0755

The **SMALLEST FLOWERING PLANT,** *Wolffia angusta,* is so tiny that two plants in flower would fit inside this letter "o." #0756

The "desert onion" Onyanga grows in the Namibia desert in Angola. It's a shrub that can live for up to **2,000 YEARS.** #0757

A mushroom in Africa, called "Lady in the veil," can be heard cracking as it grows by **HALF AN INCH A MINUTE.** #0758

African bugleweed contains a chemical that messes up caterpillars so that they turn into **BUTTERFLIES WITH TWO HEADS.** #0759

The water you drink was once **DRUNK BY DINOSAURS—** it's recycled again and again. #0760

Apollo 11, the spaceflight that took astronauts to the moon in 1969, had less computing power than a **modern cellphone.** #0761

The Arab inventor al-Jazari made the **first robots** around AD 1200! #0762

In the 1830s, Charles Babbage designed the **first computer printer** but it was not built until 2000. #0763

3D computer printers **"print" solid objects,** building up the design layer by layer from plastic. #0764

The power of computers **doubles** roughly every two years! #0765

The **first personal computer**, Altair 8000, was launched in 1975. #0766

It had no screen, no keyboard, no disk drive, no mouse, and had to be **built from a kit.** #0767

45 robots of 14 "species" live in Robotarium X, a **robot zoo** in Portugal. #0768

The **first webcam** showed the coffee pot in a university computer lab, to tell workers when the coffee was ready. #0769

There are around **17 billion devices** connected to the Internet—more than two for every person on Earth. #0770

3 MAD FACTS ABOUT MEASUREMENTS

The largest unit of measurement for distance is a **gigaparsec.** It's about 3.26 billion light years or 19,000 trillion miles. #0771

The Scoville heat unit (SHU) is used to measure the **heat of chilies.** The Trinidad Moruga Scorpion pepper has a rating of up to 2,000,000 SHU. #0772

Horsepower is used to measure the power of engines—it began when people running steam-powered vehicles paid a fee based on the number of horses they had been saved from using. #0773

4 TEENY-TINY ATOM FACTS

The number of atoms in the **WHOLE UNIVERSE** is thought to be around 10^{80}—which is 1 followed by 80 zeroes. #0774

Most of every atom is **EMPTY SPACE.** Each atom has a nucleus with electrons whizzing around it. If the nucleus were the size of a basketball, the electrons would be 20 miles away. #0775

If you took all the space out of atoms, the whole human race would be the size of a **sugar cube.** #0776

Atoms are very tiny—about **25,000,000,000,000,000,000,000,000** carbon atoms make up the lead of a pencil. #0777

10 MIND-BOGGLING MATH FACTS

If you put a single **grain of rice** on the first square of a chessboard, then two on the next square, then four, and kept on **doubling** the rice, for the last square you would need enough rice to cover India to a depth of 3 feet. #0778

The Pirahã tribe in Brazil have words for only "one," "two," and "many" so can't count **three or more objects.** #0779

Our system of 60 seconds in a minute and 60 minutes in an hour comes from the **Babylonian counting system** devised 4,000 years ago. #0780

$12 + 3 - 4 + 5 + 67 + 8 + 9 = 100$
and
$1 + 2 + 34 - 5 + 67 - 8 + 9 = 100$.
There are at least nine more sums like this. #0781

You can turn a strip of paper into a **shape with only one surface** by twisting it once and gluing the ends together. #0782

There is an infinite number of infinities. 1, 2, 3...; -1, -2, -3...; 0.1, 0.11, 0.111...; 0.1, 0.12, 0.13...; 0.1, 0.01, 0.001... #0783

A **googol** is 10^{100}, which is 1 followed by 100 zeroes. This is **larger than any number that needs to be counted.** #0784

A **googolplex** is 10^{googol}. It would take longer than the Universe has existed (around 13 billion years) to write this number out in full. #0785

The pattern of seeds in a sunflower head, the shape of a nautilus seashell, and the arrangement of leaves around a plant all follow the same spiral pattern, called the **golden spiral.** #0786

The mathematician Descartes invented the system we use for drawing graphs, using X- and Y-axes, after watching a **fly crawl over the ceiling** as he lay in bed. #0787

More than

99.9%

of all species
of plants
and animals
that have
ever existed
are now
EXTINCT. #0788

SEED FERN

CAPE LION

TASMANIAN
WOLF

DODO

5 TRULY EXTREME EXPERIMENTS

Sir Isaac Newton poked a **LARGE, BLUNT NEEDLE** into his eye to test his ideas about optics (the properties of light). #0789

Italian priest Lazzaro Spallanzani swallowed **TINY BAGS OF FOOD** attached to threads and pulled them up from his stomach after a few hours to find out how food is digested. #0790

A study in 2009 found that cows who have been given names **PRODUCE MORE MILK** than unnamed cows. #0791

By crushing lumps of amber (made from tree resin) scientists can capture tiny puffs of the atmosphere **THE DINOSAURS BREATHED.** #0792

Stubbins Ffirth, a trainee doctor, tried to show **YELLOW FEVER CANNOT BE PASSED BETWEEN PEOPLE**—he dripped vomit from fever patients into cuts on his arms, into his eyes, and even swallowed it. (Although he lived, he was wrong—yellow fever is contagious!) #0793

DAISY

3 GOBSMACKING ENVIRONMENTAL FACTS

Recycling one aluminum can can save enough electricity to power a TV for three hours, and aluminum cans can be recycled an unlimited number of times. #0794

At least **50 million acres of rain forest** are lost every year, which is as big as North and South Carolina combined. #0795

The **next ice age** is due to start in about 1,500 years, but might be delayed by climate change. #0796

A laser is a beam of light energy. Some lasers are so concentrated they can vaporize a bulldozer **1,900 YARDS AWAY.** #0797

176

Velcro was invented in 1948 after a scientist found burs (sticky seeds) stuck to his dog's fur. (Under a microscope he saw they had tiny hooks.) #0798

The **wasabi fire alarm** releases the smell of wasabi, a strong-smelling horseradish, to warn deaf people of fire. #0799

Canned food has been around since 1772, but the **can opener** wasn't invented until 1855. #0800

In 1996, an American man invented a portable, zip-up cage to hide inside to escape an attack by **killer bees.** #0801

In 2007, an American woman invented a bra that converts into two **emergency gas masks.** #0802

Sir Francis Bacon invented **frozen chicken** in 1626, but he died from a chill he caught experimenting with his method for freezing the chicken. #0803

Barcodes were designed in 1949 by Norman Woodland drawing in sand at the beach. He extended the dots and dashes of Morse code into bands. #0804

The **first submarine,** the *Turtle*, used glow-in-the-dark mushrooms to provide light. #0805

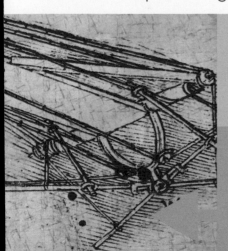

The designers of the **CD** decided it must be able to hold Beethoven's Ninth Symphony at any tempo—so CDs hold **72 minutes of music.** #0806

Leonardo da Vinci, who died in 1519, drew designs for a **tank,** a **helicopter,** a **submarine,** and a **parachute.** #0807

177

4 ROCKING FACTS ABOUT ROCKS

The **oldest known rock** is in Canada and is 4 billion years old. #0808

There are **bacteria** that live in the spaces between crystals inside rocks. #0809

Sound travels **TEN TIMES FASTER** through rock than through air. #0810

Although rubies are red and sapphires are blue, they are the **SAME ROCK**—impurities make them different colors. #0811

5 FACTS ABOUT EARTH SCIENCE

The temperature at Earth's core is over **9,300°F.** Much of this is heat left over from when Earth first formed. #0812

The **MAGNETIC FIELD** of the Earth reverses **FOUR OR FIVE TIMES** every million years, with the North and South Poles swapping over. #0813

Scientists can collect **ICE** up to **800,000 YEARS OLD** in Antarctica—and from bubbles in that ice they can sample the ancient atmosphere. #0814

INDIA was once an **ISLAND** and the Himalayas formed when it slowly crashed into Asia, pushing the edges of each landmass upward. #0815

FOSSILS of **MARINE ANIMALS** are found on Mount Everest and throughout the Himalayas, as the land that forms them was once under the sea. #0816

10 TERRIFIC TRANSPORT FACTS

A **Boeing 747** travels nearly **2 miles** on each gallon of fuel. As it can carry 550 passengers, it's more fuel efficient than most cars. #0817

Early airships were filled with hydrogen, a highly flammable gas. After some deadly explosions, helium was used instead. #0818

The **longest train** in the world was 24,114 feet long. It had eight engines and 682 wagons! #0819

The **earliest known successful flight** was by hot air balloon in Paris in 1783. #0820

The word **"juggernaut,"** a huge truck, is Indian—it's the name of a Hindu temple cart said to be used to crush people. #0821

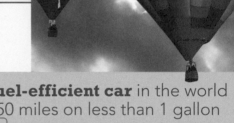

The **most fuel-efficient car** in the world can travel 250 miles on less than 1 gallon of fuel. #0822

Maglev trains have **no wheels**—they are suspended above a rail by magnetic force. #0823

In 1972, Jean Boulet landed a helicopter safely after the **engine failed** at a height of 40,800 feet. #0824

The South American Aztecs didn't make use of the **wheel,** so didn't have carts or carriages. Instead they traveled and transported things via canoe. #0825

There will be around **200,000** airplane flights in the world today. #0826

The **GREAT PACIFIC GARBAGE PATCH** is a floating mass of around 110 million tons of plastic waste and chemical sludge that has collected in the Pacific Ocean. #0827

When you're **sitting still,** you're actually **moving!** #0828

That's because Earth rotates at **1,038 miles per hour** and moves around the Sun at **66,661 miles per hour.** #0829

Then the solar system moves at **43,500 miles per hour** through the galaxy, and the galaxy spins at **492,126 miles per hour.** #0830

10 FANTASTIC FACTS ABOUT FORCES

When you jump, you exert a **tiny force on Earth,** shifting it very slightly in space. #0831

Light doesn't always travel in straight lines—it can be bent by gravity, so it curves around planets and stars. #0832

Pigeons navigate using special brain cells that detect the strength and direction of magnetic fields. #0833

A full bottle **breaks more easily** than an empty bottle. #0834

A **feather** and a **bowling ball** dropped at the same time on the **Moon** would reach the ground together. #0835

Every object has **its own gravity.** #0836

A ship trapped in a **freezing sea** would be crushed by the force of ice forming around it. #0837

Sleds move over **water,** not snow. Heat from **friction** melts a layer of snow and the sled glides over. #0838

If you break a **magnet** in half, each half will instantly get its own north and south poles. #0839

Planet Earth would be the size of a **marble** if it had the same gravity as a black hole. #0840

5 SUPER-SMART ROCKET SCIENCE FACTS

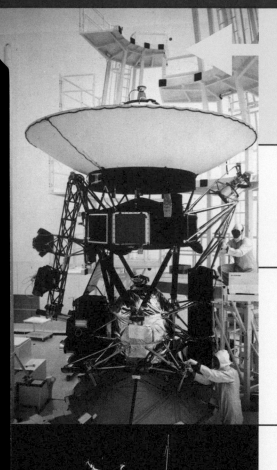

Since 1977, the unmanned spaceships **VOYAGER 1 AND 2** have been heading into outer space carrying a message for any aliens they meet. #0841

If you could convert the heat energy from a space shuttle's **ROCKET BOOSTERS** to electric power, two minutes could supply all the power needed by 87,000 homes for a day. #0842

The spacecraft **ROSETTA** will land on a comet in 2014. It weighs 220 pounds on Earth, but low gravity on the comet will reduce its weight to a **SHEET OF PAPER.** #0843

The U.S.S.R. put an unmanned lander on **VENUS** in 1970. The U.S. has still not landed a craft on the planet. #0844

There are **375,000 POUNDS** of human junk on the Moon, including abandoned and crashed spacecraft and two golf balls left by an astronaut. #0845

Americans make up **5%** of the world's population but use **25%** of the world's energy.

#0846

10 UNSTABLE FACTS ABOUT CHEMICALS

MERCURY

Mercury is the only metal that is a **liquid** at room temperature. #0847

Polonium-214 lasts less than a fifth of a second before half of it has changed into lead. #0848

98% of the normal matter in the Universe is **hydrogen** and **helium.** #0849

Stars crush together **hydrogen** and **helium** under huge pressure, making all other chemical elements. #0850

In 2006, scientists developed a material that could one day be used to make **invisibility cloaks!** #0851

Common salt is made of sodium and chloride, both of which are dangerous to humans on their own. #0852

In 2008, scientists in Mexico discovered a way of making tiny **diamonds from tequila,** by heating it to 1472°F. #0853

Oobleck is a paste of water and cornstarch. If you slap it hard it feels almost solid, but if you put your hand into it slowly it is liquid. #0854

Berkelium, a silvery-white radioactive metal, is the rarest element on Earth. Only 0.04 ounces have been made since 1967. #0855

Super-alloys are made by adding a tiny amount of one metal to another. #0856

4 EARTH-SHAKING DINOSAUR FACTS

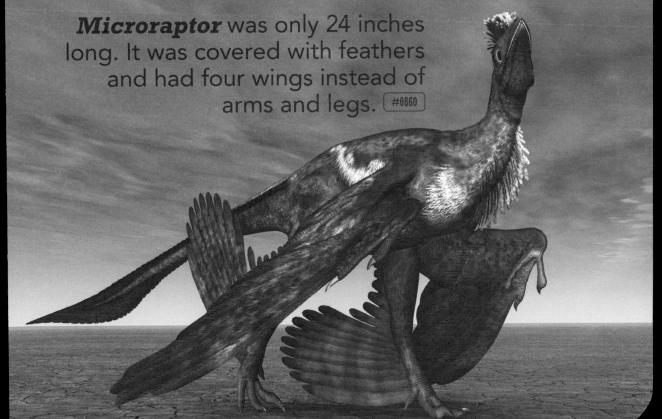

The ferocious **Tyrannosaurus rex** might have been covered with fluffy **feathers!** Lots of dinosaurs were feathered. #0857

Dinosaurs ruled the Earth for more than **TWICE AS LONG** as they have been extinct. #0858

A baby pterodactyl is called a **"flapling."** #0859

Microraptor was only 24 inches long. It was covered with feathers and had four wings instead of arms and legs. #0860

A beam of sunlight usually appears white, but actually it's made up of **LOTS OF DIFFERENT COLORS.**

If the beam happens to hit raindrops on the way down at the right angle, the colors separate so that we can see them—creating a rainbow. #0861

4 FACTS TO SEND YOU HOT AND COLD

The iceberg that sank the *Titanic* was made from the snow that fell over Greenland **3,000 years ago.** #0862

The temperature on the surface of the Sun is over **9,900°F,** but the center of Earth is even hotter. #0863

A **microbe** known just as "strain 121" lives in holes under the sea that pour out water at temperatures of **250°F**—much hotter than boiling water. #0864

Nothing can be colder than **ZERO KELVIN (-459°F).** #0865

10 FACTS ON THE HISTORY OF SCIENCE

Early doctors put **maggots** into wounds to eat decaying flesh, helping the wounds to heal. #0866

The Ancient Greeks thought a camel mating with a leopard produced the **giraffe!** #0867

2,600 years ago, Buddhist philosophers suggested that all matter is made of **atoms.** Modern physics has reached the same conclusion. #0868

Centuries ago, doctors in India would let an **ant** bite through the edges of a wound then snap off its head, leaving the jaws to act as a stitch. #0869

The first important **dinosaur fossils** were found by a 12-year-old girl, Mary Anning, in 1811 in Dorset, England. #0870

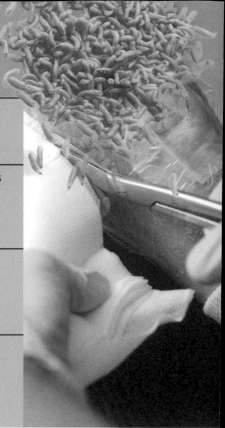

In 1947, an American engineer invented the **first microwave,** which was over 6 feet tall! #0871

Scientist Robert Bunsen suffered **partial paralysis** and **lost an eye** in an explosion in 1840 when he was researching toxic and explosive compounds called cacodyls. #0872

In 1746, a scientist sent an electric charge along **1,640 yards of wire,** held by 200 monks. All the monks yelled at the same time, showing electricity moves very quickly! #0873

The **giant squid** was thought to be legendary until it was photographed in 2004. #0874

A scientist trying to extract **gold from urine** discovered **phosphoros** by mistake in 1669. #0875

Forensic science can be used to help solve criminal cases. In the case of **FORENSIC ENTOMOLOGY,** scientists examine insects found in and around human remains to determine the time of death, or even if the body has been moved! #0876

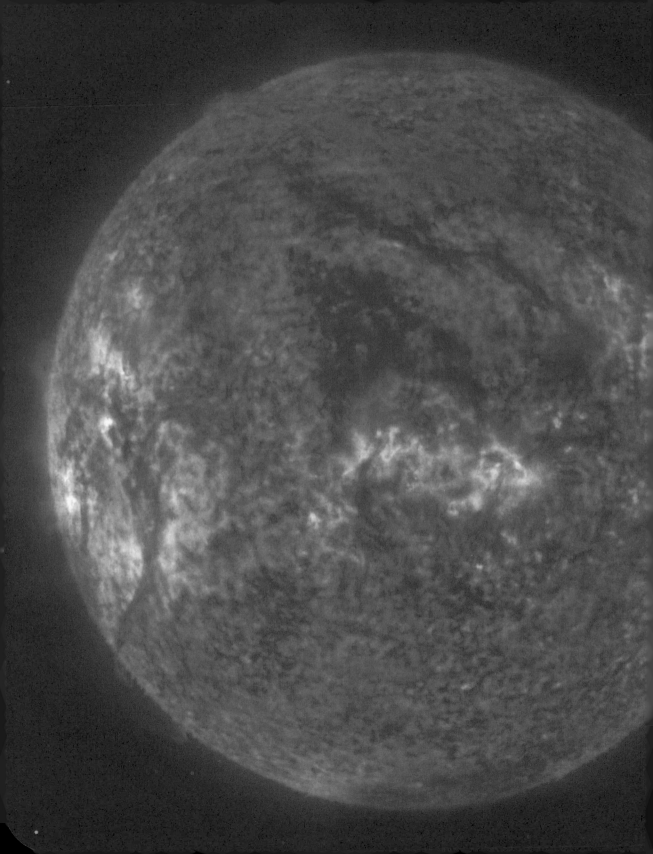

Chapter 7

EXPLORING SPACE

The **SUN** is so huge, **1.3** million Earths would fit inside it.

#0877

Planet Earth is not **perfectly round,** but actually bulges in the middle. #0878

A satellite uses very little energy— about as much as **two ordinary light bulbs.** #0879

A rocket needs to travel at **25,000 miles per hour** to escape Earth's gravity. #0880

194

10 GLOWING FACTS ABOUT THE MOON

Human footprints on the Moon will last for **millions of years,** because there is no wind to blow them away. #0881

The largest crater on the Moon is the South Pole-Aitken basin, almost **1,500 miles across!** #0882

There are **no noises on the Moon,** because there is no air to carry sounds. #0883

Since there was no wind, the American flag planted on the Moon by astronauts was **held straight with wire.** #0884

Only **12 people** have walked on the surface of the Moon. No one has been there since 1972. #0885

The Moon is moving away from Earth at the rate of just over **1 inch a year.** #0886

Moonlight takes **1.25 seconds** to reach Earth. #0887

We only ever see **one side of the Moon** from Earth. #0888

Temperatures on the dark side of the Moon fall to **-279°F**! #0889

Most scientists believe the Moon formed when a **collision** broke off a chunk of Earth. #0890

The planet Saturn is so light, it would **FLOAT ON WATER.** #0891

5 HOT FACTS ABOUT THE SUN

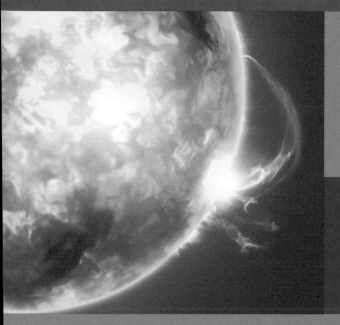

Sunlight takes **EIGHT AND A HALF MINUTES** to reach Earth, traveling at 186,000 miles per second. #0892

Fountains of flame **LARGER THAN EARTH** shoot from the surface of the Sun. #0893

Dark spots on the Sun called **SUNSPOTS** can measure 50,000 miles across—larger than the planet Uranus. #0894

The temperature at the center of the Sun is **150,000 TIMES HOTTER** than boiling water. #0895

The Sun contains **99.8%** of all the matter in the solar system. #0896

Mercury's atmosphere is so thin that if all of it was collected it wouldn't fill a **party balloon.** #0897

Mercury and Venus are the only planets that have **no moons.** #0898

The weight of Venus's atmosphere would **crush you instantly.** #0899

A **day** on Venus lasts longer than its **year.** #0900

Venus is called **"Earth's evil twin,"** because it is a similar size but hostile to life. #0901

Olympus Mons on Mars is the **tallest volcano in the solar system.** It stands three times the height of Mount Everest. #0902

The surface of Mars is icy-cold, with temperatures that rarely rise above **freezing,** even in summer. #0903

The Grand Canyon on Mars is **twenty times wider** than the Grand Canyon in Arizona. #0904

Earth is the **only planet** we know of in our solar system that humans can live on. #0905

About **71%** of Earth's surface is covered by water. #0906

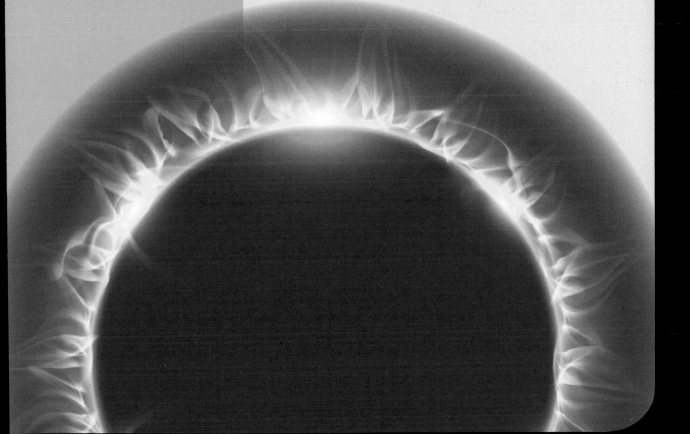

The **longest eclipse of the Sun** lasts no more than seven and a half minutes. #0907

Stars are **different colors** depending on how hot they are. The hottest stars are blue, medium ones like our Sun are yellow, cooler stars are red. #0908

In space, **blood rushes to your head,** making your face appear puffy. #0909

4 FACTS ABOUT CRAZY COMETS

COMETS speed up as they approach the Sun, to over **1 MILLION MILES PER HOUR.** #0910

A **comet** is a ball of ice and dust. As it shoots through space a comet's tail always points away from the Sun. #0911

The longest comet tails are over **6 MILLION MILES LONG,** resembling a streak of light across the sky. #0912

Halley's Comet appears every **76 years.** It will next be seen in 2061. #0913

5 FACTS TO ROCK THE GALAXY

Scientists believe there are over **100 BILLION GALAXIES** in the Universe. #0914

The galaxy nearest to our own is the **ANDROMEDA GALAXY.** Starlight from this galaxy takes 2 million years to reach us. #0915

The Milky Way and Andromeda Galaxy may collide in about **5 BILLION YEARS' TIME** to form one huge galaxy. #0916

All the stars in a galaxy are held together by **GRAVITY.** #0917

The Milky Way is estimated to be around **13.2 BILLION YEARS OLD.** #0918

Your skin would **inflate like a balloon** if you entered space without a spacesuit. #0919

Saturn's famous rings are made of **millions of chunks of rock and ice.** #0920

The Sun is about **halfway** through its 10 billion-year lifetime. #0921

10 WOW FACTS ABOUT OUTER PLANETS

Jupiter spins **faster than any other planet.** A day there only lasts about ten hours. #0922

The giant Red Spot on Jupiter is a **whirling storm** that has been raging for at least 300 years. #0923

Jupiter is **so huge** that all the other planets in the solar system would **fit inside it.** #0924

Jupiter has the **most moons** of any planet—at least 63. #0925

There are a total of seven rings, made up of **millions of ice crystals,** orbiting around Saturn. #0926

Saturn is the **lightest planet** in the solar system—it is mostly made up of hydrogen and helium. #0927

Seasons last over **20 years** on the planet Uranus. #0928

Uranus is **tilted on its side** so one of its poles always faces the Sun. #0929

Neptune has howling winds **ten times stronger** than those on Earth. #0930

Neptune's moon, Triton, is one of the **coldest places in the solar system**, with a temperature of -391°F. #0931

5 SECRETS OF THE UNIVERSE

In 2012, a British space scientist used a special math equation called the **DRAKE EQUATION** to predict that we have four intelligent alien civilizations in our galaxy. [#0932]

Instead of "little green men," the scientist also predicts that they may look like **SOCCER-FIELD SIZED JELLYFISH,** with onion-shaped limbs and an orange underbelly! [#0933]

In 2011, astronomers discovered a star that they believe is composed **ENTIRELY OF DIAMOND.** It measures 37,000 miles across—five times the size of Earth. [#0934]

Earth may have **FOUR MORE MOONS.** In 1986, a scientist discovered an asteroid in orbit around the Sun that appeared to be following Earth. Since then, at least three similar asteroids have been discovered. [#0935]

Earth is **NOT FLAT**—but **THE UNIVERSE MIGHT BE!** Using Einstein's Theory of General Relativity and scientific measurements, scientists believe it is. [#0936]

The things we know—planets, stars, galaxies, black holes—make up just **4%** of the Universe.

The rest is unknown stuff—**23% DARK MATTER** and **73% DARK ENERGY** that scientists still can't really explain. #0937

10 SMASHING FACTS ABOUT METEORS

Over a **million meteors** (shooting stars) will burn up in Earth's atmosphere today. #0938

Rock from a **meteorite** sells for as much as gold. #0939

A meteorite that fell 65 million years ago probably caused the **extinction of the dinosaurs.** #0940

Some scientists believe **life arrived on Earth** on a meteorite. #0941

Asteroids are **giant space rocks.** The largest, Ceres, is 590 miles across. #0942

Over **40,000 shooting stars** fell in 20 minutes during a meteor shower in 1966. #0943

In 1954, an American woman was seriously injured when a meteorite **crashed through her roof.** #0944

An **Egyptian dog was killed** when it was struck by a meteorite in 1911. #0945

In 1908, a meteorite broke up, causing a **gigantic fireball** that flattened 80 million trees. #0946

Earth is **getting heavier each year,** because of the meteorites and other space debris that crash here. #0947

4 LOST FACTS ABOUT BLACK HOLES

A black hole is born when a dying star collapses in an **EXPLOSION** called a **SUPERNOVA.** #0948

A black hole **sucks everything nearby into it.** Nothing can escape from a black hole, not even light. #0949

In a black hole, **time virtually stops.** That's because time goes more slowly as gravity increases. #0950

If you fell into a black hole your **BODY** would be **STRETCHED LIKE SPAGHETTI.** #0951

The **LARGEST METEORITE EVER FOUND** fell in Namibia, South Africa, in 1920. It weighed over **66** tons—as much as **15 ELEPHANTS.**

Distances between stars are measured in **light years** (the distance light travels in a year—about 6 trillion miles). #0953

Stars called **supergiants** are 70 times larger than our Sun. #0954

Our nearest star, Proxima Centauri, is 4.3 light years away—about 25 trillion miles. #0955

The brightest stars in the Milky Way shine 5 million times brighter than the Sun. #0956

In 1974, scientists searching for life on other planets beamed a message at a group of stars. It will take **25,000 years** for the message to arrive, and **50,000 years for any reply.** #0957

A rocket traveling at the speed of the Apollo spacecraft would take **900,000 years** to reach Proxima Centauri. #0958

Stars appear to **twinkle** because of varying air currents in Earth's atmosphere. #0959

Our galaxy, the Milky Way, contains at least **100,000 million stars.** #0960

The Milky Way is shaped like a spinning **Catherine wheel firework.** #0961

Many stars come in **pairs.** Planets orbiting twin suns have two sets of sunsets and sunrises. #0962

10 SHINING STAR FACTS

4 FACTS ABOUT ANIMAL ASTRONAUTS

In 1957, a Russian dog named Laika became the **first animal to orbit Earth.** Unfortunately, Laika did not survive her trip. #0963

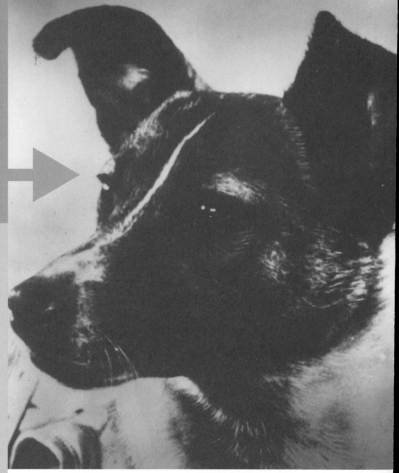

Animals that have traveled in space include **mice, a rabbit, a frog, and a tortoise.** #0964

French scientists planned to send a **CAT CALLED FELIX** into space in 1963, but he escaped. A replacement, Félicette, made the trip instead. #0965

The **first monkey in space** was called Albert II. Albert I sadly died before he got to take a trip. #0966

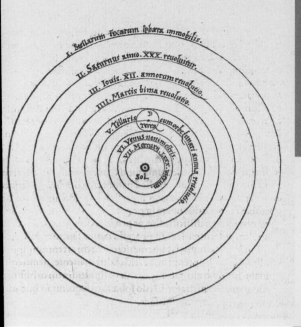

5 FACTS ABOUT EARLY IDEAS OF SPACE

In around 260 BC, Greek astronomer Aristarchus of Samos suggested the Sun was **THE CENTER OF THE SOLAR SYSTEM.** It took 1,800 years to prove he was right. #0967

In the 1600s, you could be **THROWN IN PRISON** or even **TORTURED** for suggesting Earth was not the centre of the solar system. #0968

In 1543, astronomer Nicolaus Copernicus claimed the planets **MOVED AROUND THE SUN.** His book was banned until 1835. #0969

People believed the skies were unchanging until sixteenth-century astronomer Tycho Brahe noticed a **NEW STAR IN THE SKY.** #0970

The word **COMET** comes from the Greek, for "long-haired," as they were once thought to be **LONG-HAIRED STARS.** #0971

The Apollo spacecrafts took three days to reach the Moon.

At this speed it would take a rocket

96 YEARS

to reach the planet Neptune, the most distant planet in the solar system.

#0972

10 FACTS ABOUT SPACE EXPLORERS

The **first manmade object to orbit Earth** was a Soviet satellite called Sputnik in 1957. #0973

Soviet cosmonaut Valentina Tereshkova became the **first woman in space** in 1963. #0974

In 1961, Soviet cosmonaut Yuri Gagarin became the **first man in space.** #0975

On July 20, 1969, the Americans landed **the first man on the Moon.** #0976

Neil Armstrong was the **first man to walk** on the Moon's surface, but Buzz Aldrin took the first pee on it. #0977

In 1970, the crew of Apollo 13 **nearly died** when an oxygen tank explosion crippled their craft. #0978

In 1986, space shuttle Challenger **exploded** seconds after takeoff. #0979

The American Moon landing program cost **$25 billion**—the cost today would be around $148 million. #0980

In 2012, the American probe Voyager 1 became the **first manmade object** to leave the solar system. It was launched in 1977. #0981

The rocks collected from the Moon by the Apollo astronauts weigh a total of **842 pounds.** #0982

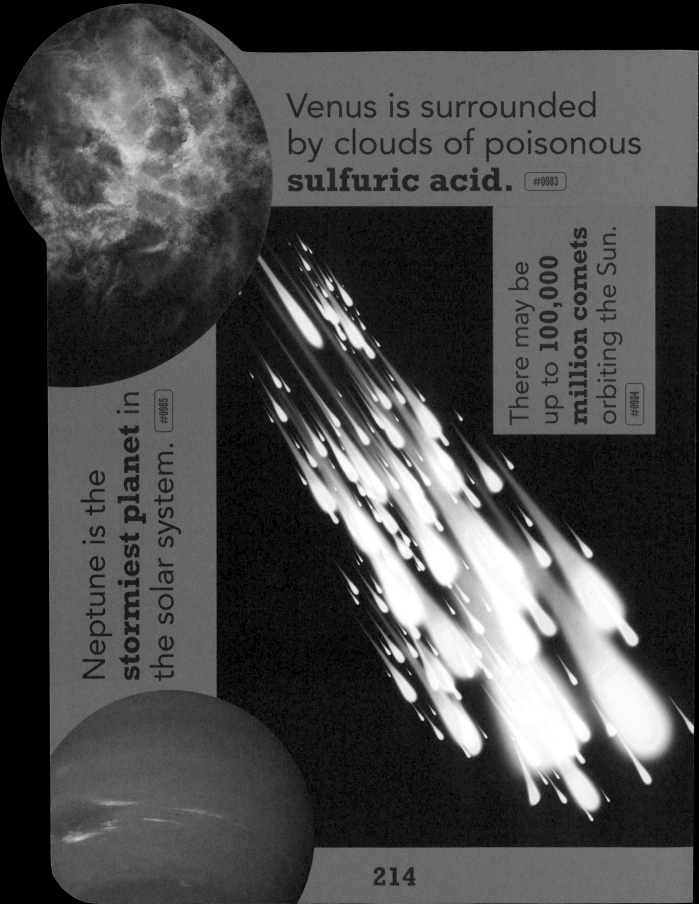

Venus is surrounded by clouds of poisonous **sulfuric acid.** #0983

There may be up to **100,000 million comets** orbiting the Sun. #0984

Neptune is the **stormiest planet** in the solar system. #0985

4 SPACE-TASTIC INVENTIONS

Smoke detectors were used on a space station in the 1970s. `#0986`

Silvery **SPACE BLANKETS** used by marathon runners were invented when 1960s scientists discovered that metal film used in satellites kept people warm. `#0987`

The **CORDLESS DRILL** was first invented to gather rock samples on the Moon. `#0988`

The world's **largest telescopes** are on high mountains in Hawaii, where the thin air allows for a great view of the stars. `#0989`

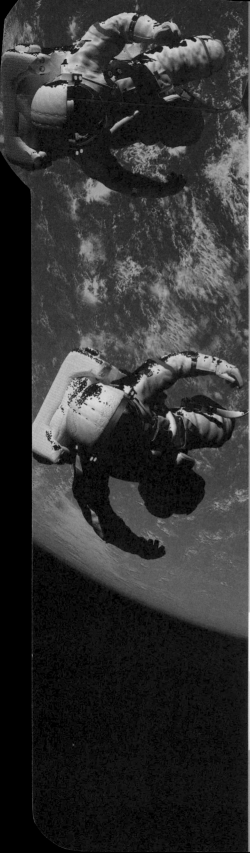

10 FACTS ABOUT LIFE IN SPACE

Russian cosmonaut Sergei Krikalev has spent **over two years** of his life in space. #0990

You get a little taller in space because there is **no gravity** to squash your bones. #0991

Astronauts living in space exercise for at least **two hours** each day so their muscles don't waste away. #0992

When in space, astronauts have to **strap themselves onto the toilet!** #0993

When they go to the toilet, a **vacuum cleaner** is used to suck up waste. #0994

Astronauts on board space shuttles saw **16 sunrises** and **16 sunsets** a day because the shuttles orbited Earth 16 times in 24 hours. #0995

It takes a day to prepare for a **walk in space,** to allow the body to get used to the environment. #0996

Space-walking astronauts wear **adult-size diapers.** #0997

Astronauts use the **Vomit Comet,** which simulates weightlessness and encourages nausea, to prepare for zero gravity. #0998

The **Olympic torch** once flew on a space shuttle. #0999

TELESCOPES are a bit like **TIME MACHINES.**

The most powerful telescopes can look back in time, seeing stars as they were millions of years ago. #1000

INDEX

ACKNOWLEDGMENTS

t = top, b = bottom, l = left, r = right, m = middle

Cover images Shutterstock.com.
Images courtesy of Dreamstime.com, iStockphoto,
Getty Images and Shutterstock.com.

Getty Images
8tr Visuals Unlimited, Inc./Ken Catania/Getty Images, 19t Barcroft
Media/Getty Images, 35 Tier Und Naturfotografi e J und C
Sohns/Getty Images, 65 FilmMagic/Getty Images, 104r SSPL/
Getty Images, 145b Planet Observer/Getty Images, 159m Tsuneo
Yamashita/Getty Images, 169 Time & Life Pictures/Getty Images,
181 AFP/Getty Images, 184 x 2 images SSPL/Getty Images, 190b
Carrie Vonderhaar/Ocean Futures Society/Getty Images, 210
Getty Images, 213mr Getty Images, 213b Michael Dunning/Getty
Images.

Shutterstock.com
9 Stanislaw Tokarski/Shutterstock.com, 13 Dmitry Berkut/
Shutterstock.com, 63 Jamie Roach/Shutterstock.com, 47 Chris
Mole/Shutterstock.com, 87 Phil64/Shutterstock.com, 103
Featurefl ash/Shutterstock.com, 105 Kiev.Victor/Shutterstock.
com, 106 Bocman1973/Shutterstock.com, 110–111 TonyV3112/
Shutterstock.com, 117 Kjersti Joergensen/Shutterstock.com, 120
x 2 images CHEN WS/Shutterstock.com, 123 Kobby Dagan/
Shutterstock.com, 129 Nicku/Shutterstock.com, 130 Eldad Yitzhak/
Shutterstock.com, 130 JeremyRichards/Shutterstock.com, 130
urosr/Shutterstock.com, 132 Andy Lidstone/Shutterstock.com, 134
chatchai/Shutterstock.com, 136 Rob Wilson/Shutterstock.com.